Public Planet Books

A series edited by Dilip Gaonkar, Jane Kramer,
Benjamin Lee, and Michael Warner

Public Planet Books is a series designed by writers in and
outside the academy—writers working on what could be
called narratives of public culture—to explore questions that
urgently concern us all. It is an attempt to open the schol-
arly discourse on contemporary public culture, both local and
international, and to illuminate that discourse with the kinds
of narrative that will challenge sophisticated readers, make
them think, and especially make them question. It is, most
importantly, an experiment in strategies of discourse, com-
bining reportage and critical reflection on unfolding issues
and events—one, we hope, that will provide a running narrative of our societies at this moment. Public Planet Books is
part of the Public Works publication project of the Center for
Transcultural Studies, which also includes the journal *Public
Culture* and the Public Worlds book series.

How to Be an
Intellectual in the
Age of TV

public planet books

How to Be an Intellectual

in the Age of TV

The Lessons of Gore Vidal

Marcie Frank

DUKE UNIVERSITY PRESS *Durham and London 2005*

© 2005 Duke University Press
All rights reserved
Printed in the United States of
America on acid-free paper ∞
Designed by Mary Mendell
Typeset by Tseng Information
Systems, Inc. in Bodoni Book.
Library of Congress Cataloging-
in-Publication Data appear on the
last printed page of this book.

For Michael Moon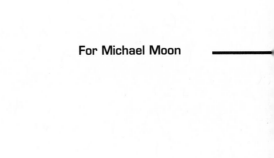

Contents

Acknowledgments

This project began as a conference paper about TV as a vehicle for sexual revolution in Vidal's *Myra Breckinridge* and *Myron*. I wrote it at the invitation of my Concordia University colleagues Tom Waugh and Chantal Nadeau, who cohosted the "Sex on the Edge" conference in Montreal in October 1998. That paper never would have become this book without the warm reception of its audience, especially Michael Warner, Michael Moon, and Jonathan Goldberg, or without the promptings, conversation, and involvement of other friends and colleagues. Amy Villarejo, my copanelist on that occasion, drew my attention to Vidal's aphorism: "Never pass up the opportunity to have sex or appear on television." In a way, the whole book was there in embryo, but its instincts needed to be unfolded and substantiated by more reading and research.

Many thanks to the people who provided friendly ears and key suggestions at timely moments, including Larry Glickman, Jill Frank, Eve Kosofsky Sedgwick, Chantal Nadeau,

Cliff Doerksen, Chuck O'Boyle, Jason Camlot, David McGimpsey, David Sheps, Harvey Shulman, and Nicola Nixon, who also provided the opportunity for another conference presentation. Michael Warner and Ken Wissoker were receptive to the idea of a book about Vidal from the get-go and helped me see how to write it in an accessible, reader-friendly way. Fred Kaplan kindly put me in touch with Harry Miller, the archivist at the Wisconsin State Historical Society, who provided me with the information I requested. Miranda Campbell has been the ideal research assistant. Thanks to Jonathan D. Katz, who invited me to participate in a panel discussion celebrating the 55th anniversary publication of *The City and the Pillar* at the Larry Kramer Center at Yale, where I enjoyed meeting Vidal. Thanks also to Concordia University for providing funding for research travel and helping to defray the costs of the book's illustrations.

The crucially enabling aspect of writing this book, one that made writing it such a pleasure, was the sense that its audience would include my friends. For giving me ideas, information, hospitality, encouragement, and stylistic help, I am indebted to Bonnie Honig, Jonathan Goldberg, Rick Rambuss, Tom Perrotta, Nick Ganoudis, Mark Dow, Adam Frank, and, especially, Celina Bell. Kevin Pask patiently read more drafts than either of us cares to remember and each time was engaged and generous. He will recognize the ideas he contributed to the following pages despite their translation into my prose. My daughters, Emma and Violet Pask, have graciously accommodated my interests even when they have interfered with their own. Michael Moon has been this book's ideal reader. His writing from the position of a fan has been an inspiration to me; his friendship has licensed the emotional risks of speculation. For his unstinting generosity, I dedicate this book to him.

Introduction

N*ever pass up the opportunity to have sex or appear on television.*" If this savvy piece of wisdom, attributed to Gore Vidal, is to be believed, sex and television provide interchangeable, short-lived, orgasmic pleasures. Vidal should know. He has presumably relished the pleasures of both, using each to craft his public persona. The witty injunction packs its punch by offering a novel juxtaposition in the familiar idiom of self-help, the title of the imaginary manual from which it could have been drawn: *How to Manage Your Fame*.

Like Andy Warhol, who had TV in mind when he said in 1968, "In the future, everyone will be famous for fifteen minutes," Vidal is a grand analyst of fame in the electronic age. Warhol and Vidal register fame's fleetingness but, more significantly, prove themselves to be among its greatest managers — Warhol in the field of art and Vidal in the field of letters. Both understand television as a transmissions apparatus that links the famous with their audience in a giant circle jerk.

Although a case could be made that literary fame is Vidal's

grand topic, one that he's explored in diverse writings in multiple media over the course of a long career, Vidal himself recognizes that literary — indeed, intellectual — fame is no longer restricted to print. When assured by an interviewer that he was still a famous novelist, Vidal replied, "There is no such thing anymore," explaining that one could be famous and a novelist but not famous as a novelist.[1] This wry attitude toward the banalization of American culture and politics does not disguise his glee in the new screen forms of fame, which he exploits at every turn.

2   Vidal presumably indulges in the joint opportunities to have sex and appear on TV because he can. To date, the pleasures of both are not available to everyone. More people can find sex than can get on TV, and herein lies the appeal to those of us who might share the fantasy of getting off and getting on TV. By supposing a majority of people for whom there could never be too much of either pleasure, the aphorism turns on an exposure of the supposedly private pleasures of sex as public in orientation. Vidal's recognition that the pleasures of sex and appearing on TV are interchangeable suggests a new way to think about the problem of the intellectual.

Many accounts of the public intellectual suggest that the species is virtually extinct, yet Vidal has been a veritable fixture on the American intellectual scene for the past forty years. Paradoxically, perhaps, his ubiquity in print, in politics, and on big and small screens has discouraged the recognition of his achievements, though a few have overcome the chronic resentment of celebrity that plagues those who tally such matters. For Edward Said, for instance, Vidal is an ideal example of the intellectual; however, this is because of his position as an independent (not institutionally affiliated) expatriate. (Vidal moved to Italy in 1963, though in 2004 he returned to Los Angeles, where he has maintained a residence since 1978.) Writers like Martin Amis and Christopher Hitchens have been impressed by Vidal's success in a variety of media, while he has been almost completely ignored by the academic literary establishment. Although recent interest, academic and other, in matters of gender and sexuality has prompted a slight increase in institutional attention to Vidal, his refusal to be labeled as gay and his insistence that no identities follow from sexual practices have proved problematic for those who would include him in a gay canon. Unlike many of his contemporaries, Vidal has unwearyingly addressed the nation in his "State of the Union" essays and elsewhere, and he continues to do so even as the public has become increasingly fractured along lines of race, class, and ethnicity as well as gender and sexuality (figure 1). Vidal's idiosyncratic combination of patrician hauteur and radical politics proves as hard to assess within the framework of the American political spectrum as his attitudes toward sexuality do in the framework of current literary or cultural analysis.

Vidal has been slippery to categorize because he has consistently played against expectations. In blurring the fine line between insider and outsider, he has redefined those boundaries. Born to a family with political clout and connections, Vidal saw his economic and class privileges and expectations oscillate, however, with his mother's marriages and divorces. He practically flunked out of prep school and never went to

1. Vidal at a podium. Courtesy of Photofest.

university, having preferred to acquire a deep familiarity with classical, European, and American literature and history on his own. Vidal's autodidactism proves essential to his intellectual style.

An avowed "America firster" out of loyalty to his maternal grandfather, Thomas Gore, the first senator from Oklahoma, Vidal nevertheless enlisted in the army in 1942 at age seventeen, thus managing to both please and instill fear in his military father and grandfather, both of whom expected that he would go on to a career in politics, for which serving one's country was a requirement—ideally not from the front lines. (He never passed the officers' training test that would have allowed him a safer posting, and, ultimately, family strings were pulled to place him on an army freight-supply ship stationed in the Aleutian Islands.) Having become a novelist during the war, he wrote *The City and the Pillar* (1948), the first American novel to depict homosexual sex explicitly, yet this did not stop him from running for public office twice, first for Congress in 1960, as a Democrat in heavily Republican upstate New York, and then for the Democratic nomination for Senate in 1982, against Jerry Brown in California.

Vidal has invoked the later 1940s, the brief period of cultural openness between the end of World War II and the onset of the Cold War, with increased frequency in recent years. In the novel *The Golden Age* (2000), and in a 2003 photo-essay in *Vanity Fair*, those years are portrayed as a critical time of political and artistic possibility. Vidal has thus courted dismissal as an elder statesman who is simply nostalgic for the period of his youth. Since satirists don't normally grow nostalgic with age, it is worth asking what he is supposed to be nostalgic for.

Having doffed his uniform in January 1946, the strikingly handsome twenty-one-year-old Vidal spent the next two years writing and publishing three novels—*Williwaw* (1946), *In a Yellow Wood* (1947), and *The City and the Pillar*—and enjoying the exhilarating atmosphere of postwar Manhattan. New York City teemed with returning servicemen, and the theater, ballet, music, and literary scenes flourished. When he wasn't working as an editor for Dutton, Vidal took ballet lessons, paid for by the GI Bill, to help the circulation in his legs, having developed rheumatoid arthritis of the knees when he was drenched in the Bering Sea. He spent his evenings at clubs like the Blue Angel, hanging out with artistic celebrities, or at the bar of the Astor Hotel, picking up men.

The year 1948, in which Vidal published *The City and the Pillar*, also saw the publication of Alfred Kinsey's *Sexuality in the Human Male*, which established that one in three men had had at least one homosexual experience to orgasm. In spring 1949, Vidal gave Kinsey his sexual history in an interview conducted for Kinsey's new research on the relation between homosexuality and the arts. Vidal and Kinsey sat in the mezzanine of the Astor Hotel, overlooking the bar where so many specimens of male fitness, many still in uniform, milled about, happy to engage in the casual pleasures of male-male sex. Kinsey gave Vidal a copy of his famous report with an inscription thanking him for his "work in the field."

In a sense, Vidal's literary career took a nosedive off that mezzanine. The publication of *The City and the Pillar* prompted the *New York Times* to blackball Vidal; Orville Prescott, the *Times* book reviewer, refused to review any future novels that Vidal might write. Although Vidal tried publishing pseudonymous pulp fiction in the 1950s, he found the venture insufficiently remunerative, even though he experimented with the Dictaphone, the then-new recording machine, for efficiency in the composition of his detective trilogy —*Death in the Fifth Position* (1952), *Death before Bedtime* (1953), and *Death Likes It Hot* (1954)—published under the name Edgar Box. That pseudonym registers in print his real source of income during that time: writing for television.

There were one million televisions in the United States by 1949, and, by 1955, more than half the homes in America had one. During the decade that came to be known as television's Golden Age, Vidal wrote live TV dramas, over seventy in 1952–53 alone. Television and film offer Vidal a continual frame of reference for his writing. Recollecting the night he experienced a breakthrough in the composition of *Williwaw*, he remembers being oddly excited by a film he had seen the night before—*Isle of the Dead* with Boris Karloff. When Vidal evokes the later 1940s, he recalls a set of opportunities that were then new, including new sexual definitions and new media for expression. This conjunction is not unique to his treatment of the period.

A more middle-of-the-road example of the intellectual, often also overlooked in accounts of the public intellectual, is the liberal Cold Warrior and Kennedy adviser Arthur Schlesinger Jr. (b. 1917), one of America's most famous historians. Like Vidal, Schlesinger too is concerned with the new media and new sexual definitions in his memoir *A Life in the Twentieth Century*, even though he begins his ruminations, not in the 1940s, but a decade earlier. He recalls keeping a notebook to record the 482 movies he saw between June 1, 1931, and sometime in 1936. Like a schoolmarmish Myra Breckinridge, Schlesinger graded these films, giving Josef von Sternberg's *Dishonoured* with Marlene Dietrich a B+ and Robert Z. Leonard and P. G. Wodehouse's *Piccadilly Jim* with Robert Montgomery a B−.

Schlesinger follows the *New Yorker* writer Roger Angell (b. 1920) when he identifies those intellectuals who came of age with him as "the Movie Generation." He observes: "My enthusiasm for Gore Vidal (b. 1925) remains under control, but the first sentence of his delightful book, *Screening History* strikes a responsive chord: 'It occurs to me that the only thing I ever really liked to do was go to the movies.' "[2] Schlesinger had himself written film reviews and poetry for *Granta*, the undergraduate literary magazine at Cambridge University, where he studied on a yearlong Harvard fellowship in 1938. Notwithstanding his critique of Harvard's Anglophilia, which he detects in the Junior Society of Fellows' preference for sherry over martinis during the cocktail hour, Schlesinger, a second-generation Harvard American historian, was born and bred to academe. Perhaps it was his academic orientation that prevented him from developing a more imaginative movie-rating system and becoming the Joe Bob Briggs of his day.

Though his memoirs are peppered with plot summaries of the movies he has seen, Schlesinger can barely do more than acknowledge the influence of those movies in his banal account of how Hollywood fulfilled the national need for stories of individual potency and self-determination during the Great Depression. Summing up this digression on the movies, Schlesinger states: "For the young intellectuals of the Thirties, film replaced the novels and short stories that had so moved the young intellectuals in the Twenties" (*Life*, 142). But this opposition between page and screen crystallizes only retrospectively, with the advent of TV. Aiming for a wry note, Schlesinger observes of his notebook: "The title of the next to last flick predicted the nation's dreary destiny: a film with Mary Astor and Lyle Talbot, rated by me D+. It was called *Trapped by Television*" (140). Like Schlesinger, Vidal claims, "Today where literature was, movies are" (*Screening History*,

5), but he does not mourn the shift from print to screen. Instead, he uses it to practice the intellectual career.

An appreciation of TV and a suspicion of the institutions of higher learning are not the only things that Schlesinger's controlled enthusiasm for Vidal kept at bay. Schlesinger parades his innocence of the homosexuality of some of the people who were important to him, notably his Harvard mentor F. O. Matthiessen, describing his surprise to learn of Matthiessen's long-term love relationship with the painter Russell Cheney alongside other examples of such surprise in his father and Lionel Trilling, who told Schlesinger that, when he wrote his study of E. M. Forster in the early 1940s, he didn't know that Forster was gay (*Life*, 165–66). Strangely proud of his own lack of imagination about others' sexual interests when they are not heterosexual, Schlesinger structures his encounter with the closet so that it revolves around the familiar alternatives of knowledge or ignorance and silence or volubility. "In the Thirties," he concludes, "same-sex love, even Matty's and Cheney's, dared not speak its name. Now, as has been frequently observed, it won't shut up" (166).

If we now know better than Schlesinger about the sexual preferences of Forster, Matthiessen, and others, what exactly is it that we know? Schlesinger's celebration of the closet epitomizes one of the intractable problems with the knowledge regime of sexual definition that Vidal short-circuits when he makes the non-nostalgic claim that the sexual revolution of the 1960s really began in the 1940s. Among the things that we can't specify in terms of the knowledge that defines people by sexual orientation are the ways in which Matthiessen's sexual secret may have contributed to the cultural prestige and pedagogic charm to which his students, including Schlesinger, were powerfully attracted. In contrast to Schlesinger, in Vidal we see someone whose own wit and charm coexist with, if they do not derive from, his curiosity about and openness to others' sexualities.

Yet Vidal's own relation to the closet is vexed. Vidal has made no secret of his own sexual practices, yet he claims not to be a homosexual (because no such thing exists). To the extent that the closet names a sexual secret, Vidal cannot be said to be either properly in or properly out of it. The position that he would occupy is beside the closet. His sexual openness, so often expressed in, on, and through TV, offers an alternative view of sexual definition and sexual liberation, allowing us to see the closet as a powerful historical structure that sublimates sexuality into cultural capital of various forms (most notably camp, but also other forms of wit) that only retrospectively come to be recognized as gay.

To take seriously Vidal's proposition that TV is another erogenous zone is also to launch a new narrative of the print-screen shift. The difficulties in accounting for Vidal as an intellectual have everything to do with the ways in which debates about the intellectual have been framed. Many accounts of the intellectual describe television as a decimating plague. Intellectual elitists mistake uniformity for quality when they prefer a slender output in a single medium over multiple appearances across media. Debates about the public intellectual rarely have anything to do with sex. Vidal's career displays the ways in which the media shift of the past fifty years from print to electronic modes of publicity has reshaped what counts as an intellectual. A consideration of the example of Vidal makes it possible for descriptions of the intellectual to catch up with reality.

Throughout the 1960s and 1970s, Vidal made numerous television appearances, promoting his books on talk shows, and in other capacities as well. While other literary writers of his generation, like Updike, Bellow, Baldwin, and Roth, barricaded themselves in book chat, Vidal took the full plunge into the new media age. He served briefly as guest host for David Susskind's talk show *Open End* in 1963, and, in 1976–77, he also appeared—as himself—in six episodes of Norman Lear's experimental soap satire *Mary Hartman, Mary Hartman*, in which he collaborated with Mary (Louise Lasser) on a book about her trials and tribulations. Episode 153, in particular, underlines Vidal's successful management of the coalescence of print and screen forms of fame by showing him springing Mary from her confinement in the mental hospital with a strategically placed phone call: capitalizing on his network connections, he promises Ackerman, the hospital administrator, an appearance on the David Susskind show in exchange for Mary's release (figure 2).

Vidal continues to write for big and small screens. In 1989, he wrote the made-for-television movie *Gore Vidal's Billy the Kid*, starring Val Kilmer, and, in 1990, an unproduced screenplay for Martin Scorsese based on the life of Theodora and Justinian. As of this writing, Vidal is adapting his *The Best Man* for a new movie version. (The successful stage play was

2. Vidal plays himself on *Mary Hartman, Mary Hartman*.
Courtesy of Photofest.

initially produced in 1960 and revived on Broadway in 2000;
the first film version, directed by Franklin Schaffner and starring Henry Fonda and Cliff Robertson, was first screened at
Cannes in 1964.) Although he has not appeared much on
TV since the early 1980s, he made a number of film appearances in the 1990s. In Tim Robbins's mock documentary
Bob Roberts (1992), he took the part of Brickley Paiste, the
liberal incumbent senator from Pennsylvania whose reflections on American imperial ambition, coming out of the First
Gulf War, remain relevant (figure 3). Paiste is defeated by
Roberts (played by Robbins), the folksinging businessman-
cum-politician, who baits Paiste as lily-livered.

More recently, in the dystopian 1997 sci-fi flick *Gattaca*
(directed by Andrew Niccol), Vidal played the director of

3. Vidal as Senator Brickley Paiste. Courtesy of Photofest.

a space-explorations plant, a role that initially would seem more of a dramatic stretch. That film's mediocre message— "There is no gene for the human spirit"—unfolds from a murder investigation that threatens to derail the successful passing of an "imperfect" or de-gene-erate astronaut (Ethan Hawke) who infiltrates the highest ranks of Vidal's institute despite the fact that his conception was unplanned. The other all-too-human figure in the movie is Vidal as the murderous director. Until his crime is detected (he spat in the eye of his victim, thereby leaving infallibly detectable traces of his handiwork), the director denies his guilt, calmly shrugging as he states to the investigators: "You can check. I haven't a violent gene in my body." The banal irony of this proclamation of innocence by the guilty party is deepened and rendered more amusing as uttered by Vidal, whose vested interest in countering genetic determinism is readily available to the viewer who has read his masterpiece of transsexuality, *Myra Breckinridge* (1968).

In a sense, these performances are extended cameos: in them, Vidal is always recognizable as himself. However, Vidal is not famous merely for being famous. These appearances signify beyond the self-sufficient domain of Hollywood celebrity as instances of Vidal's use of a print-screen circuit to maintain an intellectual career. Accounts of the public intellectual have supposed such careers to be impossible primarily because they treat print and screen cultures as independent of each other, as successive epochs. By demonstrating the intermingling of print and screen modes of publicity, Vidal's career offers the ideal opportunity to suture the divide that appears to separate them.

As Vidal acknowledged to the guest host Susan Sarandon on an episode of cbs's *The Late Late Show* that aired December 19, 2004, his "State of the Union" essays evolved out of a mode of political commentary that he originally developed in appearances on *The David Susskind Show*. Vidal reverses this shift from electronic to print modes of publicity in his writing, where it appears as a constant feature: it is a crucial subject in the essays, the grounds of formal experimentation in novels such as *Myra Breckinridge*, *Duluth* (1983), and *Live from Golgotha* (1992), and the backdrop against which the seven-novel series known as the American Chronicles unfolds. This series of historical romances—*Washington, D.C.* (1967), *Burr* (1972), *1876* (1976), *Lincoln* (1984), *Empire* (1987), *Hollywood* (1990), and *The Golden Age* (2000)—dramatizes Vidal's political and historical views by mapping the shift from American Republic to American Empire onto the shift from print to screen cultures. The historical novels thus provide the theory of his intellectual career, while the experimental novels provide the practice.

Those who embrace Vidal as an exemplary intellectual tend to foreground his essays and historical novels. However, I propose that his survival as an intellectual has depended on his negotiation of the shifts between print and electronic modes of publicity by tactics most visible in *Myra Breckinridge* and its sequel, *Myron* (1974). In these novels, Vidal presents television offering a radical opportunity to solve the world's problems: it is the vehicle through which history can be altered and the sexes revolutionized. The advice never to pass up the opportunity to have sex or appear on television is one of the lessons of Gore Vidal on how to be an intellectual in the age of TV.

1   The Print Intellectual

I t may seem strange to us that the paradigmatic intellectual was once so literary. It takes an effort to recall that the novelist sat at the top of this heap, especially considering that, for the most part, being a novelist today does not qualify you as a consultant on much of anything. But scientists like C. P. Snow, philosophers like Jean-Paul Sartre, and literary critics like Edmund Wilson and Lionel Trilling all wrote novels. Commenting on the fate of the novelist in the age of the screen in *Screening History*, the book that delighted Arthur Schlesinger, Vidal remarked:

> Recently I observed to a passing tape recorder that I was once a famous novelist. When assured, politely, that I was still known and read, I explained myself. I was speaking, I said, not of me but of a category to which I once belonged that no longer exists. *I* am still here but my category is not. To speak today of a famous novelist is like speaking of a famous cabinetmaker or speedboat designer. How can a novelist be famous, no matter how

well known he may be personally to the press, when the novel itself is of no consequence to the civilized, much less to the generality? (2–3)

Vidal has exploited electronic forms of publicity, from tape recorders to televisions, both to stay famous and to address the divergence of the categories *literary author* and *intellectual*. Even though he considered himself first and foremost a novelist, he realized "in the black winter of 1953 . . . that the novel as a popular art form had come to a full halt, [that] the most colourful [of his fellow serious novelists] was writing unsuccessful musical comedies, the most talented had virtuously contrived to die, others had dropped from view, finding dim employment in anonymous journalism or in the academy, the cleverest ones ha[ving] married rich wives."[1] Under these conditions, Vidal committed himself to writing for the camera.

Those of Vidal's literary contemporaries not struggling to uphold the primacy of print at all costs made forays similar to his into the newer media. Norman Mailer, Truman Capote, Jacqueline Susann, and Susan Sontag not only made television appearances on talk shows; they also wrote for the screen. Mailer and Sontag even ventured to direct their own films. None, however, has more ably negotiated the shift from print to screen than Vidal, even though some of these contemporaries have been held in higher literary regard. His success stems, in part, from his always appearing in print and on-screen in the most thinly disguised versions of his always recognizable self. Yet Vidal's embrace of the media of celebrity has not vitiated his political credibility; it would be difficult to come up with another example of a current writer with as much.

A brief comparison here is instructive. When Sontag went to Sarajevo in 1993, she directed a production of Samuel Beckett's *Waiting for Godot*. Exerting her political commitments in the name of culture, she went, in other words, primarily as a literary or cultural figure. Her mode of political engagement was based on an older, print-based model of the intellectual, one familiar from the days of the *Partisan Review*, where in 1963 she had initially published *Notes on Camp*, her springboard into the public eye. Indeed, Sontag might have been the last of the breed whose print orientation permitted a double commitment both to cultural elitism (traditional standards, avant-gardism, and a celebration of high modernism) and to leftist politics.

Recent critiques of Sontag's political engagements as a writer-intellectual by Bruce Robbins, Carl Rollyson, and Lisa Paddock vent a fair amount of hostility toward her without registering the source of disappointment in the fact that the position of the writer-intellectual is no longer sustainable in the media age.[2] Edward Said, for example, places Sontag in the company of the men whom Russell Jacoby dubbed "the last intellectuals," all a decade or more older than she, including Philip Rahv, Alfred Kazin, Irving Howe, Daniel Bell, William Barrett, and Lionel Trilling.[3] Vidal is closer in age to this group than Sontag was, but simply to imagine him in this list is immediately to register the lack of fit: his groomed elegance is completely at odds with the rumpled tweedy look of those academic types who, moreover, disdain appeals to a televisual public. The gender difference displays itself in the difference between Vidal's flair, which would seem to be the very thing that disqualifies him as an intellectual, and Sontag's glam seriousness, which counted in her favor. But Vidal has been disqualified equally from the ranks of the pop intellectual by broadcasting issues of sexuality beyond the stylistic range of embodiment offered by Mailer's machismo, Capote's camp effeminacy, and Susann's drag queeniness.

Accounts of the decline of the public intellectual want to neutralize questions of style, but they remain in their thrall. Much as they bemoan the disappearance of a general mode of address, one that transcends style even though it is epitomized by print, and by the novel at that, they find causes for this disappearance in the university or television. They remain blithely unaware of the circularity of their own logic: the assumption that the venue for the intellectual must be print determines that the shift from print to screen has signaled the intellectual's demise. Their hostility to screen modes of publicity, particularly television, and to celebrity more generally, has made it difficult for them to recognize the persistence of intellectual possibilities in a career like Vidal's.

Vidal specified what he could achieve with TV writing in 1956:

> With patience and ingenuity there is nothing that the imaginative writer cannot say to the innocent millions. [Television drama] is particularly satisfying for any writer with a polemical bent; and I am at heart a pro-

pagandist, a tremendous hater, a tiresome nag, compla-
cently positive that there is no human problem which
could not be solved if people would simply do as I advise.
(*United States*, 1158)

What he has understood about solving the world's problems
is intimately connected with what he has learned about screen
cultures—both film and TV screens—especially about their
relations to print cultures. His use of the screen to transmit
his views can make it appear that he has abandoned print and
the novel, but this is not the case. Vidal's treatment of the decline of the novel reminds us that the general mode of address
may simply have shifted from print to electronic venues. It is
worth reconsidering both the narratives of the decline of the
intellectual and the narratives of the decline of the novel in
the light of his career.

The Decline of the Intellectual?

On August 1, 1999, the *New York Times Education Supplement* reported the formation of "Public Intellectuals," a new
PH.D. program at Florida Atlantic University in Boca Raton.
This program, which "combines interdisciplinary humanities studies with practical training in the art of the public persona," would seem to suggest that the best the university can
do these days is to offer its graduates supplemental training in
negotiating market conditions, a mission that horrifies some
academics but has been embraced by others. Teresa Brennan, who designed the curriculum, is cited in the article's

final paragraph: "At the very least, the successful doctorates will lead 'a much more satisfying life than they would have as frustrated professor[s]' " (7). Brennan's program promises to alleviate the frustration that, in an update of the old maxim, "Those who can, do; those who can't, teach," she construes as the norm of professorial existence. But this frustration might be better understood as symptomatic of the uncertainty about the place and function of the university since the later 1980s.

It has become difficult to separate the debates over "the public intellectual" from the debates over the university and its curricula (particularly in the humanities) that have since come to be known as the *culture wars*. Paradoxically, the same cultural climate that produced attacks on "tenured radicals," prescriptions for cultural literacy, and the defunding of humanities research also prompted the attempt to resituate the intellectual work associated with the university more visibly in the public domain. These attempts to recuperate the public intellectual by academics and nonacademics alike are hampered, as the case of Vidal suggests, by an unwillingness to see the ways in which the university's relation to the public has been systematically reconfigured as part of a larger discursive transformation from print to electronic modes of publicity.

Richard Posner's recent *Public Intellectuals* gives a succinct, though strictly quantitative, account of the decline of the public intellectual.[4] Posner argues that the marked increase over the past fifty years in the specialization of knowledge has contributed to the disappearance of a sufficiently educated general readership, a public with enough knowledge of history, economics, politics, literature, science, and law to distinguish good from bad "public intellectual goods," thus increasing the appetite for them. On the supply side, this specialization has contributed to the disappearance of independent intellectuals and their replacement by academically affiliated public intellectuals, though there is no necessary correlation between the caliber of the latter's scholarship and the quality of their work as public intellectuals. Posner thus clarifies an inverse ratio: more specialization correlates with more public intellectual goods produced by those less equipped by training for those less prepared to evaluate them. For Posner, then, university affiliation is a symptom rather than a cause of decline.

For Edward Said, by contrast, university affiliation is closer to a cause, and the remedy that he recommends, now that being an independent intellectual is no longer an option, is the cultivation of an amateurism that he describes as a requirement for intellectual productivity. On the flip side, Bruce Robbins portrays a natural fit between the professionalism of professors of literature and intellectual, political, or public engagement. Although they take opposite positions on the hospitality of the university toward intellectuals, neither Said nor Robbins fully acknowledges the links between the specialization of knowledge and the media shift. Their accounts can thus sound nostalgic for a print-based intellectual culture, a problem that Posner avoids. Though he also tells a story of the decline of the educated and competent citizen, Posner incorporates into his account electronic modes of publicity.

Posner retains the basic, somewhat circular definition of

an intellectual as someone whom other intellectuals regard as such from a 1971 survey called "How and Where to Find [the] Intellectual Elite in the United States," though he expands the criteria used to measure intellectuals from frequency of publication in journals deemed elite by academics to include frequency of citation in the Lexis-Nexis database.[5] This incorporation of electronic resources, whose citational criteria include "media mentions," however, reflects Posner's minimalist conception of culture, deriving from having the market as his primary conceptual tool. Though Lexis-Nexis processes transcripts of TV and radio news and information programming, it does not collect citations on sitcoms or dramatic programming. The episode of *The Simpsons* featuring George Plimpton, for example, goes unarchived. Posner's reliance on Lexis-Nexis thus suggests that his problematically narrow understanding of culture verges on a most simplistic formulation: culture as information goods.

If Robbins, in particular, too quickly equates culture and politics in his advocacy of professionalism as the remedy for decline in intellectual engagement, Posner's understanding of culture solely in terms of the market for information is too limited from a different direction. A note to Posner's discussion of George Orwell's *1984* observes, "Orwell wrote another great political satire, *Animal Farm*" (*Public Intellectuals*, 9 n. 16), making you wonder who could possibly be in his intended audience. Although Posner treats literary criticism as the preeminent genre for public intellectuals, neither of his two exemplary practitioners of the genre, Richard Rorty and Martha Nussbaum, are literary critics. Perhaps Posner's strange sense of literature, its critics, and its readers bespeaks an investment, after all, in the print-based model of the intellectual as a hallmark of personal cultivation or taste. But his investment is tokenism rather than nostalgia, for he is more interested in the future than in the past — probably a good thing since his sense of the literary tradition is strikingly impoverished.

Because Posner sees public intellectuals only in terms of a market, the reason that he gives for their "decline" is the absence of controls on quality in this marketplace. Among the declinists, then, he thus stands apart from the claim that it is TV (as the epitome of market culture) that has eviscerated public discourse.

The title of Neil Postman's 1985 *Amusing Ourselves to Death* nicely conveys the mortal consequences that Postman argues follow from the replacement of print by television as the predominant medium of our culture.[6] Like Postman, Pierre Bourdieu holds TV accountable for the decline of public discourse in his 1996 *On Television*.[7] Like Postman, he invokes Plato's location of the philosopher apart from the agora to describe true intellectual debate as that which is marked by its independence from the market. For Postman, Bourdieu, and others, the problem posed most acutely by TV is the future of intellectual and political discourse. But this purported decline contrasts TV's reliance on market values to a presumed detachment of the intellectual, or of print discourse, from the market. In these accounts, TV's market orientation retrospectively purifies print from the taint of the market. But print never was independent from the market. Print can come to

look pure compared to TV by means of the same fantastic revisionary process at work in the 1980s, when the flooding of
the drug market by crack cocaine made heroin more palatable
to the middle classes.

Most accounts of the public intellectual invoke Michel
Foucault's description of the "specific" as opposed to the
"universal" intellectual. Whether they adhere to or critique
Foucault's understanding of power, these invocations of the
"specific" intellectual share with Foucault the sense that Enlightenment universalism is no longer viable.[8] Enlightenment

universalism and its codification of knowledge acquisition in
the terms of humanism have been the main stakes in the debate between the defenders of the traditional university curriculum and the proponents of the university as a relevant
political space. But it has not been adequately recognized by
members of either camp that Foucault's contrast between the
specific and the universal intellectual turns on the changed
cultural status of the writer:

> The intellectual par excellence used to be the writer: as a
> universal consciousness, a free subject, he was counter-
> posed to those intellectuals who were merely *competent
> instances* in the service of the State or Capital — techni-
> cians, magistrates, teachers. Since the time when each
> individual's specific activity began to serve as the basis
> for politicisation, the threshold of *writing*, as the sa-
> cralizing mark of the intellectual, has disappeared. The
> whole relentless theorisation of writing which we saw in
> the 1960s was doubtless only a swansong. Through it, the

writer was fighting for the preservation of his political privilege; but the fact that it was precisely a matter of theory . . . proves that the activity of the writer was no longer at the focus of things.[9]

Foucault perceives that the waning of the writer as an exemplary intellectual figure must be central to any account of the intellectual. It is from the point of view of the changed status of the writer that Foucault addresses the role that the universities have played as the intellectual's new location:

> It has become possible to develop lateral connections across different forms of knowledge and from one focus of politicisation to another. . . . This process explains how, even as the writer tends to disappear as a figurehead, the university and the academic emerge, if not as principal elements, at least as "exchangers," privileged points of intersection. If the universities and education have become politically ultrasensitive areas, this is no doubt the reason why. And what is called the crisis of the universities should not be interpreted as a loss of power, but on the contrary as a multiplication and reinforcement of their power-effects. (*Power/Knowledge*, 127)

Foucault goes on to identify a range of other possible sites for the specific intellectual, including the courts, the prison, and the hospital. His distinction between the universal and the specific intellectual, like Posner's treatment of the specialization of knowledge, can help us see why the university has become implicated in the debate about intellectuals. Moreover, his attention to the status of print culture in the genealogy of the intellectual suggests that, in their nonengagement with the media shift, both defenders of the traditional university curriculum and proponents of what has been called *political correctness* may have equated too quickly the project of a humanist education with universalism.

Foucault had Jean-Paul Sartre in mind as the last of the universal intellectuals when he located the emergence of the specific intellectual as a post–World War II phenomenon. This temporal frame is intriguing since it offers a longer view than do those accounts that locate the switch point between the universal and the specific intellectual in the 1960s, when specific identity formations, articulated by the civil rights and women's rights movements, entered the political arena.[10] Foucault's account of the demise of the universal intellectual after World War II invites us to let the postwar period and the status that it accorded to the writer shape the story of the advent of identity politics and to correlate such changes with the media shift from print to electronic modes of publicity, especially from 1945 on, when television became more and more of a household device.

Current accounts of the intellectual, whether nostalgic or celebratory, have worked within, rather than analyzed, the problematic relation of culture and politics, a problem that manifests itself most acutely in their weddedness to a print-based model of the intellectual career. Foucault invites us to factor the writer back into the story of the intellectual, yet, when we turn to the writers who reflect on the impact that the newer media have had on the cultural status of the novelist, it turns out that, like the historians of the intellectual, they too begin in the 1960s.

The Decline of the Novel?

David Foster Wallace's wittily entitled "E Unibus Pluram" charts the influence of television on writers born in (or after) the 1960s in order to address the changed cultural status of the novelist in terms of the media shift and the rise of identity politics. Wallace claims: "The most dangerous thing about television for U.S. fiction writers is that we don't take it seriously enough as both a disseminator and a definer of the cultural atmosphere we breathe and process."[11] The really interesting questions about television — what we hate about it and why we are so immersed in it if we hate it so — are being asked, according to Wallace, only in certain strands of American fiction and by television itself.

There are a number of salutary features of "E Unibus Pluram." Unlike Postman, Bourdieu, and company, Wallace worries about discussing TV in a paranoid register. He thus identifies and avoids the two pitfalls that most treatments of TV fail to navigate: demonization, on the one hand, most evident in the reactionary vocabulary of those who hold TV responsible for the lowering of aesthetic and moral standards, and salvation, on the other, visible in the claim that the problems caused by TV technology can be resolved technologically. Wallace's fairly evenhanded treatment of "the television whose weird pretty hand has my generation by the throat" (49) is what distinguishes him from his friend Jonathan Franzen, for whom TV certainly does represent the lowering of aesthetic standards.

In the 1996 *Harper's* essay "Perchance to Dream," Franzen called for a revitalization of the "social novel," which had become difficult for white men to write because of television and the fracturing of the American social body along lines of gender, class, and ethnicity.[12] According to Franzen, women writers and those of an ethnic minority have been enabled rather than hampered by these conditions, though he does not explain the uneven impact. When Oprah Winfrey selected his novel *The Corrections* (2001) for her book club, Franzen expressed his concern that this opportunity to boost his book's sales might interfere with its reception as "high" art, and Oprah dropped him from her list. Though more sympathetic to TV than Franzen, Wallace sees the mission of the contemporary novelist as providing different and better aesthetic, moral, and intellectual options than those available on TV.

Wallace offers a persuasive analysis of the ways in which TV has conditioned the mode of irony available in postmodern writing that he calls *the finger*. As he clarifies:

> What explains the pointlessness of much published TV criticism is that television has become immune to charges that it lacks any meaningful connection to the world outside it. It's not that charges of nonconnection are untrue but that they've become deeply irrelevant. It's that any such connection has become otiose. Those of us born in, say, the '60s were trained by television to

look where it pointed, usually at versions of "real life"
made prettier, sweeter, livelier by succumbing to prod-
uct or temptation. Today's mega-Audience is way better
trained, and TV has discarded what's not needed. A dog,
if you point at something, will look only at your finger.
("E Unibus Pluram," 33)

"The finger" allows Wallace to generate an important distinction between the metafictional self-referentiality that is some-
times associated with postmodernism and the post–World
War II shift in "how Americans chose to view concepts like
authority, sincerity and passion in terms of our willingness to
be pleased" (59). However, the literary history that Wallace
goes on to offer is strangely skewed:

> In terms of literary history, it's important to recog-
> nize the distinction between pop and televisual refer-
> ences, on the one hand, and the mere use of TV-like
> techniques. The latter have been around in fiction for-
> ever. The Voltaire of *Candide*, for instance, uses a bi-
> sensuous irony that would do Ed Rabel proud, having
> Candide and Pangloss run around smiling and saying
> "All the best, the best of all worlds" amid war-dead,
> pogroms, rampant nastiness, etc. Even the stream of
> consciousness guys who fathered Modernism were, on a
> very high level, constructing the same sorts of illusions
> about privacy-puncturing and espial on the forbidden
> that television found so effective. And let's not even talk
> about Balzac. (45)

Not much intervenes in Wallace's literary history between Balzac, the "dirty realism" of Joyce, and the post-Nabokovians (among whom Pynchon and DeLillo are favored for their prescience) and their experimentalist heirs of the 1980s and 1990s. This neglect of the most prominent American writers of the 1940s, 1950s, and 1960s, including Mailer, Updike, Baldwin, Roth, and O'Connor, reflects the insularity of M.F.A.- and literary-program training. Ironically, the acute perception that the appeal of TV, most evident in certain commercials, lies in the pitch, "It's better to be inside the TV than to be outside, watching" ("E Unibus Pluram," 56), finds its strongest support, not in Pynchon or DeLillo, but in a writer whom Wallace ignores: Gore Vidal, who dramatizes this same insight in *Myron* and again in *Live from Golgotha*. *Myron* is set inside the television, and, in *Live from Golgotha*, television comes to constitute the archive of history and memory.

In an essay on F. Scott Fitzgerald, for whom he otherwise exhibits no fondness, Vidal quotes with admiration Fitzgerald's observation (in the 1936 essay "Pasting It Together") of a cultural change that no one else seemed to have noticed: "As long past as 1930, I had a hunch that the talkies would make even the best-selling novelist as archaic as silent pictures" (*United States*, 296). Vidal arrived at this conclusion himself a decade after Fitzgerald and fifty years before Schlesinger. He has frequently since complained about the demise of the serious novel and about the modernist enshrinement of experimentalism that is its symptom. Vidal allows us to track the changing cultural status of the novelist as a central part of the story of the intellectual by going back to the 1940s, as Foucault asks us to do, with the additional benefit of side-lining the distracting question of the university and the exclusive and idiosyncratic recent literary history that its literature programs enshrine.

Referring to his own pronouncements on the demise of the novel, Vidal writes:

> When I wrote that the film had replaced the novel as the central art form of our civilization, I was attacked for having said that the novel was dead and I was sent reading lists of grand new novels. Obviously, the serious novel or art-novel or whatever one wants to call the novel-as-literature will continue to be written; after all, poetry is flourishing without the patronage of the common reader. But it is also a fact that hardly anyone outside of an [academic] institution is ever apt to look at any of these literary artifacts. Worse, if the scholar-squirrel prevails, writers will not be remembered for what they wrote but for the Cautionary Tales their lives provide. Meanwhile the sharp and the dull watch movies; discuss movies; dream movies. Films are now shown in the classroom because it is easier to watch Pabst than to read Dreiser. At least it *was* easier. There is now some evidence that the current television-commercial generation is no longer able to watch with any degree of concentration a two-hour film without breaks. (*United States*, 297)

Though Vidal often narrates the decline of the serious novel, his account always situates the status of print in terms of the media shift from print to electronic modes of publicity. Although his attitudes toward this shift vary, he also consistently signals an awareness that print culture never was independent of the market. His practice of the intellectual career thus offers a good perspective on the current public function of the intellectual in the age of TV because, though he technologically updates the matrix out of which the intellectual initially emerged, his writerly sensibilities, especially as a satirist, remain in many respects those of the eighteenth century, the period in which the literary marketplace first developed.

In a more optimistic moment, Vidal identified in the 1965 essay "Writers and the World" the television talk show as offering exciting new opportunities for the beleaguered novelist. He notes that American romantic puritans, first thrilled by the misbehaving artist, then satisfied by his subsequent suffering and punishment, "prefer their serious writers obscure, poor, and, if possible, doomed by drink or gaudy vice" (*United States*, 43). However, television has altered the old stereotypes, opening up new possibilities for writers. The talk shows need writer-celebrities partly because their producers realize that they can be interesting when they talk extemporaneously, unlike actors, who need scripts, and politicians, who will promote their own platforms. Vidal portrays television as bringing to novelists a new, young audience, even if it is an undereducated one. Television introduced the possibility of worldliness to writers without spelling their ruin. As the talking writer comes increasingly into contact with the world, Vidal prognosticates: "Only good can come of the writers' engagement in public affairs. At last, other voices are being heard, if only late at night on television" (47). Although

Vidal's initial optimism about the fate of the writer in the age of TV later flagged, in this essay the decline of the serious novel expands rather than contracts the writer's access to public and political debate.

Curiously, in "Writers and the World," Vidal had attributed to Mary McCarthy exemplary status as a writer-celebrity when he applauded the appearance of writers on television: "Mary McCarthy is no less intelligent a literary critic because she plays games on television. But even if her work should show a sudden falling off, only the simplest moralist would be able to link her appearances as a talking writer to her work as a writing writer" (*United States*, 46). This treatment of McCarthy can look odd in hindsight, especially in view of her 1980 *Ideas and the Novel*. Although, with the publication of *The Group* (1962), she had achieved a fair amount of public recognition, in *Ideas and the Novel* she decried the decline of the serious novel, which she blamed on Henry James's development of an "inward turn" that divested the novel of ideas. Vidal responded to McCarthy's argument obliquely, in an appreciation of Thomas Love Peacock published that same year in which he questioned the connections that McCarthy drew between ideas and the stature of the novel. Indeed, he happily bid farewell to the serious novel, which, "written by middle-class, middlebrow whites, political activists, intellectuals and members of the ruling classes," should, he advised, be taken over and manufactured on university campuses (*United States*, 148–49). Vidal here exhibits no fondness for the serious novel; rather, he professes his interest in what people will read once they are out of school. These essays suggest that it would be a mistake to see Vidal as uniformly disappointed with a decline in status of the literary author; instead, he is keenly and pointedly disappointed about the decline in literacy. Ever the proud autodidact, Vidal here regrets that reading is now increasingly done on assignment, determined by the design of university curricula.

Vidal's example ought to forestall a premature embrace of those dearly loved and hallowed narratives of decline of the serious novel. Such a narrative, however, is also one to which he repeatedly gives voice. For example, he ends the 1986 "The Bookchat of Henry James" with a lament for life in a "postliterary" age:

> In our postliterary time, it is hard to believe that once upon a time a life could be devoted to the perfecting of an art form, and that of all the art forms the novel was the most — exigent, to use a modest word. Today the novel is either a commodity that anyone can put together, or it is an artifact which means nothing or anything or everything, depending on one's literary theory. No longer can it be said of a writer, as James said of Hawthorne in 1905: "The grand sign of being a classic is that when you have 'passed,' as they say at examinations, you have passed; you have become one once for all; you have taken your degree and may be left to the light and the ages." In our exciting world the only light cast is by the cathode-ray tube; and the idea of "the ages" is, at best, moot — mute? (*United States*, 176)

Vidal's pun is overstated, particularly in view of his own voluminous publication. Moreover, his appreciation of James cannot be separated from his sense of his own cultural status. Though Vidal expresses the same opinions found in other accounts of the decline of the serious novel, what he does under these conditions differs.

"The Bookchat of Henry James" begins by invoking a dinner given by President and Mrs. Theodore Roosevelt at which James, who had reviewed a book by TR, was a guest. Vidal exploits the irony that the two great men meet at the table "not as literary lion and president but as book reviewer and author reviewed" (*United States*, 168), an irony appropriate for a review of James's book reviews, one that aims to give the literary man the upper hand that he already has in print at the dinner table as well. Noting Henry Adams's absence from this dinner, a non sequitur in the context of this review, allows Vidal to bring his own fiction into subtextual relevance, for this scene is referred to but not dramatized in his novel *Empire*.[13]

Empire treats the youth of Caroline Sanford, who is adopted as a "niece" by Adams. Her half brother, Blaise, spawns Peter and Enid Sanford, the main characters of *Washington, D.C.* Caroline's experiences span the disaggregation of the Gilded Age's sociopolitical sphere of power centered in Washington, which Vidal outlines by tracing her movements from Washington, as a newspaper magnate, to Hollywood, as a movie star and would-be film producer. As the "center of consciousness" of *Empire* and its pair, *Hollywood*, Caroline Sanford is Vidal's most Jamesian heroine—she has even met the Master in *Empire*. Vidal considers *A Portrait of a Lady* "as nearly perfect a work as a novel can be" (*United States*, 178); his Isabel Archer, however, has, of necessity, explicit, rather than oblique, relations to money and sex. Caroline's magnetism exerts a pull on her author as well as on the characters who surround her; like Myra Breckinridge's, Caroline's voice took him over, not once, but twice. Vidal even told his biographer, Fred Kaplan, that "he couldn't let [Caroline] go" and that *Empire* and *Hollywood* should be considered two halves of the same novel.[14]

Vidal is a satirist with a direct political agenda. As such, his literary endeavors would appear to be strikingly at odds with James's representational investment in individual conscious-ness. There are plenty of reasons, however, for Vidal to cast his literary ambitions in Jamesian terms apart from aesthetic admiration for James's achievements, including the fact that both have patrician family histories and live, or lived, much of their lives as expatriates. Vidal's reorientation of James's sig-nature indirection might seem like a necessary consequence of the shift from Republic to Empire, from print culture to screen culture, from a literary life lived in the reflected light of the ages to one lived in the light cast by the cathode-ray tube.

However, Vidal's apparent nostalgia for the light of the ages is complicated by his incarnation of the boob tube itself in Myra Breckinridge. In the novel to which she gives her name, and in its sequel, *Myron*, Vidal presents TV as the vehicle for altering gender, sexuality, and, ultimately, history as well. Moreover, in *Myron*, Vidal affiliates the debonair man behind the scenes of MGM studios, the black Mr. Williams and his desire for the destruction of the studio system so that print can regain its lost primacy, with the literary enterprise of the late James. Intoning, "The golden bowl has begun ever so slightly to most beautifully crack," Mr. Williams repeatedly offers this metaphor for the ruin of the studio system that Myra works so assiduously to restore.[15] In a sense, Myra, celebrant of screen media, and Mr. Williams, mourner of lost literary possibility, stand in for two parts of Vidal himself.

In Vidal's practice of the intellectual career, both parts are equally important. His consistent treatment of the decline of the novel in terms of the media shift works across the print-screen divide. Vidal does not idealize a world of print free of market considerations, nor does he demonize the newer media because they are market driven. Indeed, his main complaint about both print and electronic media is their being subject to censorship. Vidal has discovered that he can remain a universal intellectual and retain the general mode of address available to those novelist-intellectuals of his generation, who today would be classified according to their areas of disciplinary expertise, by supplementing the role of the writer with television. But his use of screen media, both big and small, flies in the face of most accounts of their cultural impact.

The talk show, one of the most durable genres and a staple of TV programming from its earliest days, would seem a likely candidate for cultural content on television, as Gore Vidal points out in "Writers and the World." Indeed, one of Vidal's best-known TV appearances was on a 1971 episode of *The Dick Cavett Show* that featured Norman Mailer and Janet Flanner as the other guests (figure 4). The hostility between Vidal and Mailer, which dominated the entire show, periodically threatened to erupt into fisticuffs. Both Flanner and Cavett entered the verbal fray, which came to a climax when Cavett told Mailer to stick the piece of paper on which he had listed his complaints about Vidal "where the sun don't shine." If it is difficult to imagine a literary battle supplying such a vibrant piece of theater today, this is less because talk TV has changed than because literary rivalry has barely any cultural consequences.

Only in 1977 did *The Dick Cavett Show* move to PBS, where it aired until 1982. Originally, it had been broadcast late at night on ABC from 1969 to 1972 (figure 5). In April 1972, ABC,

4. Vidal and Mailer appear on a special hour-long edition of
The Dick Cavett Show. Courtesy of Photofest.

which was running behind CBS and NBC in late-night viewer-
ship, threatened to cancel the show if ratings did not improve
by July. The resulting controversy was almost unparalleled in
TV history. ABC was inundated with more than fifteen thou-
sand letters running nine to one in favor of the *Cavett Show.*
Several ABC affiliates ran "Save *The Dick Cavett Show*" advertisements, and notable public figures urged that the show be
continued, which it was until 1974. One highbrow show, the
Cavett Show would seem to have offered a venue for the intellectual that wasn't print.

Yet it has become commonplace to blame TV, in particular the talk show, for the decline in public discourse. Some
people complain of this decline as it is represented by the air-
ing of formerly private problems on shows like *Oprah, Phil*

Donahue, and *Jerry Springer*. But the current therapeutic orientation of talk television could simply be seen as a recapitulation at a mass level of Andy Warhol's selection of the television over the therapist in his account, in *The Philosophy of Andy Warhol*, of the purchase of his first TV. Recounting how he "started an affair" with his television in the late 1950s, Warhol bought an RCA nineteen-inch black-and-white on the way back from a visit to a psychiatrist and promptly forgot all about the psychiatrist, who, in any case, never called him back

5. Dick Cavett.
Courtesy of
Photofest.

6. Joe Pyne.
Courtesy of Photofest.

for a follow-up appointment.[1] If TV now no longer seems like a viable alternative to therapy, this is because therapy-speak has pervaded all venues.

Other people take the confrontational style memorably incarnated in the 1980s by talk-TV host Morton Downey Jr. as a symptom of a recently debased political debate, but this interview approach was pioneered much earlier by Mike Wallace, who hosted two shows in the late 1950s and early 1960s: *Night Beat* and *The Mike Wallace Show*.[2] Indeed, Downey had been anticipated by Joe Pyne, a chain-smoking ex-marine, who raged on his eponymous show against pacifists and homosexuals (figure 6). On an episode that aired during the Watts riot, a militant black guest noted that Pyne, living in a safe middle-class neighborhood, didn't have anything to fear. Pyne responded by opening a desk drawer to reveal a gun, at which point the guest drew back his coat to reveal that he too was armed. Another episode featured Pyne driving Lee Harvey Oswald's mother to tears.[3]

Vidal and Mailer's fight on *Cavett* extended the battle that had begun in print when Vidal accused Mailer of being a misogynist. In "Feminism and Its Discontents," a review of *Patriarchal Attitudes* by Eva Figes in the July 22, 1971, issue of the *New York Review of Books*, Vidal linked Mailer with Henry Miller and Charles Manson, branding this version of patriarchal privilege with the logo of industrial capitalism, 3M.

The status of women in the vocabulary of the women's movement permeated all discussion that night on *Cavett* right from the start — the opening interview with Flanner. Discussing life in France, Flanner mentioned de Gaulle's absolute certainty that the students could not overthrow the state in 1968. When Cavett asked how one gets to be absolutely certain about anything, Flanner replied: "It helps to be male." At least since the 1960s, women's struggles have helped redefine the relations between the public and the private, an observation that prompted a 1990 account of talk shows to contend that shows like *Oprah* usher in a new public, one that is no longer the spectator but rather the protagonist, in the sense of being what the program is constructed around.[4] But this episode of *Cavett* lets us see that audience participation was already galvanized around women's issues in 1971. Having introduced himself as a "student of television," Mailer responded to Vidal's defense of women's liberation by standing up and asking the audience: "Why are you so hostile to me?" The response he got included boos, hisses, and catcalls of "pig . . . pig."

The *Cavett Show* did not exhibit the supposedly secure and homogeneous male domination of cultural discourse in public. Indeed, Jack Paar, the host of *The Tonight Show* from 1957 to 1962, had already broken with any pretense to hostly neutrality by displaying his own political and emotional convictions, using the show as a soapbox from which to denounce his enemies. Under the tutelage of Johnny Carson, Paar's handpicked successor, *The Tonight Show* became the prototypical talk show, the one that, now hosted by Jay Leno, continues to preside over late-night broadcasting. In at least one account

of talk shows, *The Tonight Show* is depicted as emblematic of a Hollywood ethos that stands in strong contrast to David Letterman's New York–based late-night show.[5] This familiar east-west split piggybacks on the location of New York as the cultural and intellectual center of the nation because of its dominance in older, print-based cultural forms like the theater and the publishing business. Relying on the same east-west split, the recent film *Adaptation* (2002) portrays the revenge of a Hollywood-based screenwriter on a New York–based *New Yorker* writer as he struggles to adapt her book *The Orchid Thief* for the screen. The wild inventiveness of this revenge—the screenwriter must discover that the writer is really a drug-addled would-be murderer in order for him to complete an adaptation that can thus include the amount of action, death, and gore requisite for success on film—suggests that the geographic contrast is exhausted. Meanwhile, a high modernist form of self-referentiality has finally come to Hollywood. We don't have to chasten the film for its sell-out ending, as many reviews did, if we understand Charlie

Kaufman to have penned *A Portrait of the Artist as a Young Screenwriter*. Nor does Joyce show Stephen Dedalus going on to achieve writerly fame.

The opening monologue that Cavett delivered on the episode featuring Vidal, Mailer, and Flanner offers a particularly salient view of the connections between the new access of women to the public's interest and the status of literary culture on television. Cavett stated: "A lot of critics knock TV. They think it lacks culture." He continued that "to prove to them that TV has figured in the thoughts and writings among literary professionals," he had asked his research department to survey treatments of his show in print. The results included a number of fictional examples, which Cavett produced to the delight of the audience: William F. Buckley Jr. on Cavett's low stature; Kate Millett calling Cavett "little pig, big mouth"; and, most interesting for my purposes, the galleys of a novel called *Between the Acts* that features a sex scene in which lean and bronzed participants turn off a lean and bronzed TV set that is playing the *Cavett Show*. *Between the Acts* is the title of one of Virginia Woolf's lesser-known novels (of 1941), but Cavett's writers also alluded, in an ironic and veiled fashion, to Jacqueline Susann's best-selling novel *The Love Machine* (1969). The joke stages the cultural viability of television by playing to the educated viewer's appreciation of the differences between Woolf and Susann and dramatizing the "pulpy" preference for sex over television. Although the joke sets off Woolf, as stand-in for highbrow literary culture, against Susann, as lowbrow, it is curious to note that, in an essay called "Middlebrow," Woolf took pains to defend the integrity and mutuality of high and low against the incursion of the middlebrow.[6] The joke would encourage viewers to identify as readers who, disdaining Susann (and Woolf?), leave the *Cavett Show* on, but it also exploits Susann's rendering in *The Love Machine* of the television set as a lover, "always waiting in the bedroom, available twenty-four hours a day"—here lean, bronzed, and playing *Cavett*.[7]

Vidal and Mailer's display of literary rivalry *on* TV and Cavett's representation of literary rivalry *with* TV both suggest that what was at stake in this episode's almost zoological display of types of machismo was the diminishing literary, cultural, and political authority of the male novelist. It is significant from this standpoint that Vidal himself comes to be a figure, not only *on*, but also *for* TV.

The most concise example of this figuration occurs toward the end of *The King of Comedy* (1982), Martin Scorsese's brilliant treatment of televisual celebrity. When Rupert Pupkin (Robert De Niro) ransoms the famous talk-show host Jerry Langford (Jerry Lewis) for an appearance guest-hosting his show, the lineup includes Shelley Winters, Tony Bennett, and Gore Vidal. For Scorsese, Vidal can represent "normal" TV on the verge of interruption by Rupert Pupkin by virtue of his numerous television appearances, as a guest on *Cavett* (in 1971 and again in 1973), and as an ABC commentator on the 1968 Democratic national convention in Chicago, which featured his famous confrontation with William F. Buckley Jr.

Writing TV drama during the mid-1950s offered Vidal a way to make money when he was unable to support himself as a novelist, but television writing seems also to have provided the crucial scaffolding for his longest-standing fictional enterprise, the historical novels of the American Chronicles. *Lincoln*, the most famous and probably the most highly regarded novel in the series, was first conceived for television.

A transcript of a story conference that Vidal had with the television producer Norman Lear reveals that it was in discussing how to develop throughlines linking the episodes that Vidal had put together for the TV Lincoln that Vidal hit on the idea of using John Hay, one of Lincoln's secretaries, as a sort of narrator. Vidal mused on discovering the narrative usefulness of Hay for the TV Lincoln: it is "as though we're going to see the story through his eyes even though we don't really."[8] In the novel, it is through Hay that Vidal links the writers, journalists, White House occupants, congressmen, socialites, and prostitutes of the varying social circles of Lincoln's Washington. Hay would have seemed a natural choice, having co-written with John Nicolay, Lincoln's other secretary, a ten-volume biography of Lincoln, but it is significant that it is in conference with Lear that Vidal first developed the idea.

The conference transcript ends on an interesting note. Having agreed that he will put together another treatment of the story, one that will liven up the historical material so that it "won't read dry," Vidal said: "This is known as putting in the jokes. It's always the best part of it which I like to save for when I'm really writing it, not a dress rehearsal. It's a peculiar art form." When Lear responded, "It's not an art form," Vidal replied: "It's a peculiar THING form. 'Cause it has to be clear what you're doing, and interesting, and I don't object to doing it. Normally I would. I object to it so much ordinarily that I would probably never do anything for television. But I don't mind doing it in this case because I have to do it anyway. I have to get the history straight." As the transcript reveals, working out the historical materials for television allowed Vidal to develop many of the features that he used to organize *Lincoln*. Another of Vidal's lessons for being an intellectual in the age of TV, distilled here, is that TV offers the opportunity "to get the history straight."

TV on Film

Vidal's use of TV "to get the history straight" provides a particularly interesting counterpoint to the ways in which TV has been represented elsewhere. As the example of Scorsese's *The King of Comedy* suggests, representations of TV on film provide one good map of the points between which responses to it have oscillated: paranoia and romance. Movies of the past few years like *The Truman Show* (directed by Peter Weir, 1998), *Edtv* (directed by Ron Howard, 1999), and *Pleasantville* (directed by Gary Ross, 1998) represent TV as a totalized and totalizing space. In these films, this space is represented from the inside, and, though they take pains to show the points of entry and egress from within the televisual world, these films basically argue that there is no outside. Dilating TV's panoptic gaze, they suggest that no aspect of life is too private for public interest; they thus make the point that public attention is equivalent to consumption—both activities are determined by the commercial interests that shape and measure them.

One could point to a number of factors informing recent

filmmakers' bleak sense of their audiences' potentials, including the anxiety that, with the widespread use of home video- and cable-viewing technologies, film no longer commands a separate theatergoing audience willing to access the aesthetic pleasures particular to the cinema. This demonization of TV in mainstream movies of the 1990s also owes something to the representations of TV as a threshold of horror in 1980s horror films that also addressed this anxiety. From the point of view of the late-1990s films, films from the 1980s like *Videodrome* (directed by David Cronenberg, 1983), *Poltergeist* (directed by Tobe Hooper, 1982), and *Gremlins* (directed by Joe Dante, 1984) represent an interesting Janus-faced moment, for they retain a sense of film's analytic powers and its independent audience, both bemoaned as lost by Weir and company, even as they record the threat of TV. *Poltergeist* treats TV as a domestic threat to the nuclear family ensconced in the home; *Gremlins* looks at the threat that TV poses to Hollywood; and *Videodrome* conflates anti-TV and antisex messages. Together, these films indicate the range of paranoid responses to TV.

Videodrome seems interested in the possibility that there is a life-enhancing force of television, which the McLuhanesque Brian O'Blivion's daughter, Bianca, disseminates to the disenfranchised at the Cathode Ray Mission. However, the film's most memorable scene shows Max Wren (James Woods), president of a small and controversial cable channel, developing an eerily vaginal slit in his abdomen into which pulsating fleshly videocassettes are introduced, by means of which he is programmed by Spectacular Optical, a mysterious corporation bent on eliminating the "soft" element of society. Because it concentrates most of its energies on Wren's transformation from low-level TV corporate guy to pawn, from confident seducer to dupe, from whole to penetrable and vulnerable body, the film never succeeds in differentiating adequately between the two ideologically opposed forces of O'Blivion and Spectacular Optical. The feminizing of Wren elaborates Cronenberg's extended visual pun on being fucked by television. *Videodrome* thus occupies a strange place as a text concerned with the sexual threat of television, pointing, on the one hand, to other paranoid takes on TV on film, in print, and even on TV itself and, on the other, to the romance of TV, which is much harder to trace once we move beyond the discourse that, in "E Unibus Pluram," Wallace identifies as "salvational-tech" to include other styles. Two other films about TV, *Medium Cool* (directed by Haskell Wexler, 1969) and *Network* (directed by Sidney Lumet, 1976), in conjunction with Scorsese's *The King of Comedy*, provide an important contrast to the 1980s horror movies and their 1990s rearticulations, not because they were made earlier (although some periodization is useful), but because they register the promise as well as the threat of TV and, in so doing, point to a romantic rather than a paranoid representation of the medium.

Medium Cool, with its McLuhanesque title, is the least familiar of the three. It is about a television cameraman who becomes increasingly disillusioned as he records the escalating racial and political tensions in Chicago in the summer of 1968. The film was screened in London on the eve of its rerelease on DVD, and, in a July 25, 2001, review, the *Guardian*'s arts reporter, Duncan Campbell, claimed there could be no better moment to show it. In the wake of Genoa, Seattle, Quebec, and Gothenberg, all sites at which protestors of the World Trade Organization's meetings clashed violently with police, the film's examination of the role of the media "seems ominously knowing" (16). *Medium Cool* is an exercise in cinema verité, and the film's climax—the cameraman's death in a car accident—occurs during, and because of, the violent confrontation between student demonstrators and police on the streets outside the Democratic national convention. The film's naturalist style, with little emphasis on plot and character, allows Wexler to incorporate documentary footage, including many scenes of the riots. The chant of the protestors, "The whole world is watching," provides the sound track, and the film ends with voice-over comments from a member of the press that underscore the visual message of the last third of the film: that the real action is taking place, not on the convention hall floor, but outside in the streets. Although he had been prepared to feel allied with the police against the students, the cameraman has been radicalized by the violence that he has seen and himself been subjected to (he reports having been pushed up against a wall by a cop). Thus, although earlier in the film the cameraman temporarily lost his job when he made a fuss about the TV station routinely turning over its tapes of draft-card burnings and other protests to the police and the FBI, the film ends with the sense that the world's eyes, prosthetically enhanced by television, will help guarantee that justice and equality prevail over force and brutality.

"I'm mad as hell, and I'm not going to take it anymore," the catchphrase by which TV news anchorman turned prophet Howard Beale (Peter Finch) gets America's television viewers to unglue themselves from their screens and yell out their windows, probably provides *Network* with its most memorable scene. The film turns on the paradox of delivering an anti-TV diatribe on TV. As Beale instructs a live studio audience and those watching at home later in the film: "TV is not the truth. Turn off the television." The film ends with a voice-over running over the credits, styled in the cadences of a TV newscast: "This was the story of Howard Beale, the first man to be killed because he had lousy ratings." But Paddy Chayefsky, the screenwriter, himself one of television's most talented and acclaimed writers, is equally interested in exploring television's more promising potentials. He sets the action of a corporate takeover of a fictional television station, UBS, against the romance between William Holden's Max Schumacher, the older news producer, and Faye Dunaway's Diana Christensen, the young, beautiful, but frigid embodiment of the new world of TV. The Dunaway character's strength as a producer rests on her realization that "the American people want someone to articulate their rage for them" and her ability to find footage that does so. Holden's character leaves the relationship to return to his wife in the film's penultimate scene, but an earlier exchange between Schumacher and his wife has revealed that all his behavior is governed by scripts, some of which are just more conducive to life, an insight that informs the entire film. Unlike *The Truman Show*, *Network* does not contrast the scripted aspect of human relationships to something more authentic.

Both *Medium Cool* and *Network*, unlike the paranoid films about TV, find the political promise of the medium to lie in its extensive access to its audience, even if they depict problems with a lot of what is broadcast. Both films provide interesting intersections with the career of Vidal: Wexler was the cinematographer on the 1964 film adaptation of Vidal's *The Best Man*; Vidal's battle with Buckley (as ABC's talking heads) provided a memorable moment in the televisual version of the 1968 Democratic convention in Chicago; and Vidal, along with Chayefsky and Rod Serling, helped craft what was broadcast on television during its Golden Age.

In *The King of Comedy*, Vidal indexes "normal" TV, but, if Vidal is one of the archetypal talk-show guests in that film, Jerry Lewis is anything but the archetypal talk-show host. For all Lewis's astonishing celebrity as a live act (both with Dean Martin between 1946 and 1956 and then solo) and as a film star and filmmaker, he was an unqualified flop as a TV host. Two attempts to host his own program, in 1963 for ABC and in 1967 for NBC, were both critical and popular disasters. Shawn Levy, Lewis's biographer, speculates that the anarchic energies of Lewis's live performances could not be captured effectively on the small screen.[9]

Scorsese's film brings together Vidal and Lewis, but, curiously, this odd coupling has a precedent: a 1960 film version of Vidal's stage play *Visit to a Small Planet* that starred

7. Cyril Ritchard and Sybil Bowan in the 1957–58 stage production of *Visit to a Small Planet*. Courtesy of Photofest.

Lewis. According to Lewis, it was Vidal's idea to cast him, but this seems implausible considering the lack of fit remarked by the film's few commentators between Vidal's satire and Lewis's slapstick shtick. Moreover, Lewis characteristically cast the appeal of the film to children: "There are hundreds of thousands of children who are going to see this movie —all they want to do is laugh" (figures 7 and 8).[10] Indeed, Lewis's hysterical paternalism is perhaps more familiar from his only televisual success, the astonishingly long-lived *Jerry Lewis Telethon*. Aired annually on Labor Day since 1966, the fund-raiser for muscular dystrophy has featured Lewis on the stage, talking about "Jerry's kids," for most of a twenty-one-and-a-half-hour broadcast. Levy persuasively accounts for the

8. Jerry Lewis in the film version of *Visit to a Small Planet*.
Courtesy of Photofest.

telethon's success by observing its live-ness. The telethon gave
Lewis the opportunity for "success in television, his old bête
noire, on his own terms: no network executive, no censori-
ous sponsors, no week-to-week grind of ratings, worries and
rehearsals. For a single day, all over the country, he had, in
effect, his own TV network" (*King of Comedy*, 389). Lewis pioneered for the telethon a coast-to-coast linkup of stations to
carry the broadcast that he dubbed "the Love Network," later
adopted for Christian programming by Jim and Tammy Faye
Bakker. Like Vidal's Myra, who claims that television commercials "are the last demonstration of *necessary* love in the
West," Lewis exploits the TV as an apparatus for transmitting
love.[11] Like Myra, who conjures herself into readerly focus

by invoking the appearance of her "superbly shaped breasts reminiscent of those sported by Jean Harlow in *Hell's Angels* and seen at their best four minutes after the start of the second reel" (5), Lewis has an overtly erotic relation to celluloid. As he puts it in the prologue to *The Total Film-Maker*: "I have a confession. Crazy. I have perched in a cutting room and licked emulsion. Maybe I thought more of me would get on to that film. I don't know. I do know that plumbers don't lick their pipes. With emulsion, it's easy to get turned on."[12]

Much in *The King of Comedy* turns on another directorial choice: the withholding of Rupert Pupkin's monologue, which we do not hear until the end of the film, when he stands up at the bar, arm over the TV, listening to it along with the FBI agents who will lead him off to prison when it's over. Earlier, when Pupkin makes an audiotape of his act, we see him approach the wall of his basement, which is decorated like the set of a talk show, complete with a papier-mâché Liza Minnelli, the walls papered with the smiling faces of an audience. A laugh track overwhelms most of his jokes as he keeps his back to the camera. As the camera pans slowly backward to reveal that he stands on a stage that is an enclosed box whose white walls and convex shape visually evoke the inside of a television, the effect, which equates the stage, the television, and a loving audience with Pupkin's self-enclosure, suggests that Pupkin is insane (figure 9). The film, in fact, solicits this judgment up to the end, when we hear Pupkin's monologue. At that point, we realize that he's not nuts, just mediocre. But he's also a publicity genius, and the end of the film reveals that he has managed not to have to pay the dues that

9. Rupert Pupkin inside the tube.

he's been advised by all would be necessary and instead has catapulted himself into a career as the genuine King of Comedy, no matter how poor we may find his jokes. The insularity of television is revealed not to be madness; its real problem is mediocrity.

Narratives of decline, whether about the intellectual or the serious novel, are often wedded to print at the expense of the screen even when these narratives appear on screens. Yet, like *Network*, *The King of Comedy* finds problems with the quality of what is on TV, not with the medium itself; like *Medium Cool*, it depicts a medium that continues to have underrealized its promise. Critical though they may be, these films find ways to convey TV's promise even in the absence of any instantiation of it. These three films' conviction of the medium's potentials goes against the technological determinism that underlies the paranoid critique of the medium. These films suggest that the problems do not inhere in TV itself but rather lie in the way in which TV has been used. We could say that these films take a romantic rather than a paranoid attitude toward TV. However, it would be more precise to say that they suggest that the relation between paranoia and romance may be more fruitfully understood as a dialectic rather than as a dichotomy. This is the way in which it has been used by historians, literary critics, and political theorists who describe how American culture and politics have come to be vertically organized along high/low lines and structured, until recently, in terms of a clear separation between them: culture was not politics, nor politics culture. Vidal's negotiation of the media shift agitates against the notion, prevalent both in accounts of the decline of the intellectual and in cultural studies, that the distinction between culture and politics has collapsed and provides some terms for maintaining the separation.[13]

Michael Rogin has called the vacillation between paranoia and romance in American culture a "demonology."[14] For Rogin, Hollywood is the crucible out of which the American political demonology is produced. The presidency of Ronald Reagan—the making of which Rogin calls "Ronald Reagan, the movie," the result of a collaboration between Hollywood and Washington on a filmic reimagining of a tradition of countersubversion—provides the capstone episode in this demonology. Rogin describes Reagan's frequent confusions of the real and the filmed in his use of lines scripted for the movies on political occasions throughout his presidency. As Rogin astutely notes, this confusion is equally evident in John W. Hinkley Jr.'s assassination attempt, itself inspired by Martin Scorsese's movie *Taxi Driver* (1976). This inability to distinguish what has happened on-screen and what has happened in history has prompted Vidal to dub his country "the United States of Amnesia."

Amnesia

In *Screening History*, Vidal puts this amnesia into relation with the media shift from print to screen cultures. *Screening History* begins:

> As a writer and political activist, I have accumulated a number of cloudy trophies in my melancholy luggage. Some real, some imagined. Some acquired from life, such as it is; some from movies, such as they are. Sometimes, in time, where we are as well as were, it is not easy to tell the two apart. Do I wake or sleep? (1)

The luggage of Keatsian melancholy is quickly checked at the airport, as it were. Wittily revising the high modernist complaint of Joyce's Stephen Dedalus that history is the nightmare from which one struggles to awaken, Vidal sounds an oddly Reaganesque note as he remains blithely unconcerned about whether he is asleep or awake: "For instance, I often believe that I served at least one term as the governor of Alaska; yet written histories do not confirm this belief. No matter. Those were happy days, and who cares if they were real or not?" (1).

History may be happily ignored, but it can be reviewed and revised, if not precisely remembered, through the filtering screen of the movies. Americans' ignorance of history is positively, though ironically, revalued by their familiarity with the cinema. The tantalizing proposal that the movie screen mediates history and memory reorients the psychoanalytic concept of screen memory to emphasize its cinematic aspect. Vidal puts Freud's isolated individual into a social arena — the darkened movie theater — to exploit the comic potential of the screening process. Vidal thus suggests that the velvet light trap reorganizes consciousness, not around the tragic because traumatized unconscious, but around the blurred boundaries between personal memories and the repository of what we collectively have seen at the movies.

Contending that the tenth muse, the cinema, has replaced literature, Vidal revises Freud's famous dictum, "Where Id was, there Ego shall be": "Today, where literature was movies are" (*Screening History*, 5). And the results are possibly less than salutary. Assuaging his literary disappointment by appointing himself the enunciator of the end of literature, Vidal embraces that end's comic cinematic apotheosis. If the revisionary accommodation of the page to the screen, made necessary by popular amnesia, is facilitated by video, Vidal doesn't mention it in *Screening History*.

Both Rogin and Vidal ignore television in these accounts of amnesia, but their treatments differ in other ways. Both emphasize the cinema, but, while Rogin adheres to a fairly orthodox psychoanalytic account of the film-viewing process, one in which the lone individual interacts with the projector/screen apparatus, Vidal's viewer is a preeminently social being. TV occupies a blind spot in Rogin's analysis, but, in Vidal's other treatments of amnesia, TV does have a role to play in the transfer of memory to screen memory.

Rogin notes that Reagan's career included stints as a sportscaster on radio and as a host of *GE Television Theater* in the 1950s, but it is the uncanny slippage between life and film that is central to his account of the American political demonology. Still, TV had an important, if overlooked, role to play in Reagan's political career. If it was in Reagan and his supporters' interests to promote his larger-than-life status as a film actor and as president, it was late-night reruns of his movies on television and his smaller-than-life scale on television that turned him from a B-movie actor into "the great communicator."

As early as 1968, in the essay "The Twenty-ninth Republican Convention," Vidal tuned in to Reagan's televisual appeal. He described Reagan's speech at the Miami convention as a "warm and folksy performance which Reagan projects to some legendary constituency at the far end of the tube, some shining Carverville where good Lewis Stone forever lectures Andy Hardy on the virtues of thrift and the wisdom of the contract system at MGM." Specifying the television rerun as Reagan's best venue, Vidal "suspected even then Reagan would some day find himself up there on the platform [as the Republican presidential candidate]: as the age of television progresses, the Reagans will be the rule, not the exception" (*United States*, 842–43).

According to Connie Bruck, Lew Wasserman, the founder and president of MCA-Universal until he sold the model megaentertainment company in the late 1980s, became "king of Hollywood" because he understood the potential of TV, and Reagan had a role in his ascendancy. MCA began as a talent agency, and, when Wasserman branched into TV production in 1950, the Screen Actors Guild had in place a long-standing prohibition on talent agencies producing movies because of the inherent conflict of interest in being both the agent and the employer. It planned to but had not yet adopted similar restrictions for TV production. Waivers could be sought on a case-by-case basis, but Wasserman procured a blanket waiver for his TV production with the aid of Ronald Reagan, then president of the Screen Actors Guild and one of Wasserman's first clients. Wasserman also bought up the older films from the studios and then made millions selling the rights to TV.[15] Though Wasserman does not figure in Vidal's writings, it is notable that, in *Myron*, set mostly inside the TV in 1948, Myra's mission to restore the studio system to its glory days of pre-antitrust legislation is conditioned by her awareness of the economically intertwined fates of film and TV production.

Reagan revitalized the Cold War demonology in the 1980s, and its longevity appears to have extended beyond the collapse of the Soviet Union into our own day, with the War on Terrorism. Together, Rogin's and Vidal's analyses suggest that the success of Reagan's resuscitation of the demonology was due, in part, to his familiarity with and involvement in the fashioning of the post-1940s TV-film system. As part of his legacy, the Bushes have furthered the process of deregulating American broadcasting begun under Reagan, though its ultimate outcome remains, at this point, unclear. In June 2003, under the chairship of Michael Powell (the son of Colin Powell and the appointee in 2001 of Bush Sr.), the FCC overturned a twenty-eight-year-old rule barring both the joint ownership of a newspaper and a TV station in the same city and any network from owning TV stations with a combined reach of more than 35 percent of the U.S. viewing audience. With this decision, the FCC gave the big networks more power to monopolize the news, both on TV and in print. Now that Rupert Murdoch or Ted Turner may be free to buy up more print and screen venues, it becomes all the more urgent to recognize the relations between these modes of publicity.

Vidal has, in some ways, been the anti-Reagan insofar as his own familiarity with the TV-film system informed his sense of contemporary American politics and made him, early on, such an astute analyst of Reagan. In moving across print and screen modes of publicity, he has, like Reagan, found ways to mobilize them both, though to very different ends.

If Vidal is often silent on the matter of TV, he also often registers its crucial role, however obliquely, in his investigations of the ways in which the American political landscape has been reshaped by the formidable reach of the newer media. In the recent pamphlets *The Decline and Fall of the American Empire* (1992), *The American Presidency* (1998), and *Screening History*, and in the seven-novel series known as the American Chronicles, Vidal works across the print-screen divide to show what the two media share. *The Decline and Fall of the American Empire*, Vidal's earliest pamphlet, is Gibbon in miniature aimed at a postmodern U.S. audience, one trained by TV and impatient with the pleasures of the text. But Vidal's little book also consolidates much of the literary work that he has done, providing something of an overview of his own career.

The attack on the contributions that monotheism has made to American political history is informed by Vidal's novels about early Christianity such as *Messiah* (1954) and *Julian* (1964); the depiction of the shift in American national self-conception from Republic to Empire recapitulates the highlights of his American Chronicles from *Burr* to *Washington, D.C.* Not only are the arguments of his historical fiction in evidence in *The Decline and Fall of the American Empire*, but so too are some of the wilder speculations of his "experimental" novels, such as his analysis of the evils of the multinational corporate domination of the entertainment industry in the satire of televangelism (among other things) *Live from Golgotha*; his description of the convergence of millenarianism and U.S. intelligence operations in the dystopic *Kalki* (1978); and his phantasmagoric ruminations on the consequences of the national security state in *Duluth*. If the nonfiction reveals the conjunction of the shifts from Republic to Empire and from print to screen cultures, it is the fiction that dramatizes their intersections.

Although Vidal divides his fiction into the categories *experimental* and *historical* novels, he is concerned in each with the shift from print to screen modes of publicity. The shared concern with the media shift across the oeuvre overrides Vidal's own classification and indicates that, rather than oscillating between the poles of paranoia and romance, as his own schema might suggest, he recharts their relations. Time will tell if, in the pamphlet, Vidal has found a vehicle sturdy enough both to convey the amnesiac impact of the print-screen circuit on politics and to counter that impact by consolidating an audience that will look increasingly both to print and to the Internet for alternative sources of information to the homogenized offerings of the print/broadcast networks. Curiously, the earlier treatment of the print-screen shift in the American Chronicles occurs in an entirely different genre: the historical romance.

Vidal's American Chronicles series coordinates the political shift from American Republic to American Empire with the media shift from print to screen cultures. It thus maps a westward relocation of power from New York and Washington to Los Angeles. Significantly, Vidal delivers this powerful vision of American political history in the genre of the historical romance.

Although the historical romance attained a pinnacle of prestige early in the nineteenth century with the highly acclaimed and popularly recognized achievements of Sir Walter Scott and James Fenimore Cooper, by the mid-twentieth century it had fallen to the bottom of the barrel. Robert Graves described his own *I, Claudius* (1934) and *Claudius, the God* (1935) as potboilers.[1] The historical romance would seem thoroughly discredited and retrograde, yet Vidal uses this middlebrow genre as a vehicle for his politics partly because it addresses the broadest spectrum of readers.

The choice of historical romance is also part of Vidal's critique of the literary vanguardism preferred on college campuses. The recent resurgence of historical fiction by postmodernist writers like Michael Ondaatje, A. S. Byatt, and Don DeLillo should be distinguished on the basis of this affiliation from Vidal's formally more conventional novels. It would be inappropriate to call Ondaatje, Byatt, or DeLillo *romancers*, while Vidal's novels fit more comfortably among the classic examples of the genre. As a genre of writing, romance has been key to generating historical descriptions, even if only in the capacity of being cast as history's opposite. Vidal's historical romances, many of them bestsellers, when read in the context of other bestsellers, show the functions that romance fulfills as a term supporting relations between high and low culture since the mid-1960s.

In *Hollywood: A Novel of America in the 1920s*, the penultimate novel of the American Chronicles, Vidal fittingly brings the family genealogy through which he tracks the transition from Republic to Empire to Hollywood. As Caroline Sanford, the illegitimate descendant of Aaron Burr and founder of the Hearst-inspired newspaper the *Washington Tribune*, cultivates a parallel career as Emma Traxler, a successful movie star, Vidal develops an apposition between Washington and Hollywood. The historical backdrop of the novel consists of several geographically distant but contemporaneous scandals: the Teapot Dome scandal of the Harding administration in Washington and the Fatty Arbuckle and William Desmond Taylor scandals in Los Angeles. Vidal exploits the coincident exposure of these scandals by making Caroline, at the novel's end, instrumental in bringing Will Hayes, a former chairman of the Republican Party and the nominal author of the Hayes

Code, which determined the moral limits of on-screen representation, to Hollywood. He thereby fills in an important episode in the intimately linked histories of American politics and the movies. Indeed, through Caroline's dual career, Vidal suggests that it is as much to Hollywood as to Washington that one must look to trace the political lineaments of an empire whose major medium of (self-)representation has undergone the shift from print to celluloid.

Caroline is the vehicle through which Vidal voices his argument that film supplies politics with an expanded access to the unconscious that seems streamlined to suit the needs of a growing empire:

> Caroline suddenly realized that she—and everyone else —had been approaching this new game from the wrong direction. Movies were not simply there to reflect life or tell stories but to exist in their own autonomous way and to look, as it were, back at those who made them and watched them. They had used movies successfully to demonize national enemies. Now why not use them to alter the viewer's perception of himself and the world? Thus she would be able to outdo Hearst at last. Self-pity was now replaced by megalomania of the most agreeable sort.[2]

Caroline's stunning epiphany prompts her to integrate her dual lives by embarking on a new career as a film producer. Back in Washington only to sell her half of the newspaper to her half brother, Blaise, she plays up to Hayes's presidential ambitions, thus displaying, at the novel's end, that she is more "in" the political game than she ever was before even as she relocates permanently to Los Angeles (415).

Vidal's novelistic treatment of the power of cinematic representation in *Hollywood* sets Caroline's epiphany against the backdrop of an unfolding murder mystery, the shooting death of Taylor, her director. His treatment of this backdrop suggests that *Hollywood*, the least polished novel of the American Chronicles series, might, perhaps, have been more aptly titled *Washington, Babylon* in homage to Kenneth Anger, for, in it, Vidal shares Anger's historiographic method: the narration of history as a series of scandals. Vidal also shares with Anger a point of intense childhood identification in Max Reinhardt's 1935 film *A Midsummer Night's Dream*. In *Screening History*, Vidal's identification with the young Mickey Rooney playing Puck allows him to explore his own missed career opportunity as a child star. Anger's actual child–stardom consisted of his appearance in that film as the Indian boy, the bone of contention between Titania and Oberon. In *Hollywood*, Vidal adopts a number of salacious suggestions that Anger makes about the Taylor murder in *Hollywood, Babylon* (1975), including the identification of the murderer as Charlotte Shelby, the jealous mother of Mary Miles Minter, Taylor's young lover.[3] Dramatizing snippets of Anger's trash elegy for lost glamour, Vidal puts novelistic flesh on the bones of that catalogue of scandal. To a certain extent, then, this late-twentieth-century historical romance resembles some of its earliest precursors — the eighteenth-century satirical scandal chronicles by Delarivier Manley, including *The New Atalantis* (1709) and *Rivella* (1714). This resemblance suggests the debt that Vidal's historical novels owe to romance, a debt whose analysis allows us to traverse from his fiction, to his political writings, to his screen writing, to his public appearances on big and small screens.

Vidal's writings project an odd pantheon into which they implicitly introduce their own author. This pantheon is drawn from a range of literary levels and includes those illustrious writers of the past whom he frequently discusses, such as Nathaniel Hawthorne, Willa Cather, William Dean Howells, and, especially, Henry James, and his less canonical contemporaries about whom he also has less to say (though he says it no less trenchantly), including Harold Robbins and Jacqueline Susann.

So often taken as a deplorable symptom of market-oriented literary production, romance writers have in Vidal's fiction refreshingly different functions. Readers of *Duluth*, that fanciful experiment, will recall that each of the characters populating the archetypal American city either is a romance writer or derives from the imagination of one. Vidal's satire on the impoverishment of American culture is itself delivered in the stylistic register of romance—the novel's *mise-en-abyme* structure offers no alternative vocabulary. The romance writer, the gossip columnist, the screenwriter, and other prototypical "bestsellers" populate the American Chronicles.

When Charles Schermerhorn Schuyler, the narrator of *Burr* and *1876*, turns Hawthorne's sneer at that "damned mob of scribbling women" against him, invoking "that dark veiled lady of New England letters, Nathaniel Hawthorne,"[4]

Vidal uses this reversal to signal the failure of such efforts, both Hawthorne's and Schuyler's, to elevate genteel literary ambitions above those of "hacks," mainly women. Indeed, Vidal calls into question these efforts at self-differentiation by means of which Hawthorne and Schuyler would catapult themselves into the illustrious company of a masculine American literary tradition. Noting that Henry James disliked his friend William Dean Howells's representations of ladies, Vidal dismantles the gendered hierarchy of literary form and audience when he playfully overrides James's ambivalence toward popularity by suggesting that James himself wrote for lady readers (*United States*, 173). In his extravagant appreciation of *The Golden Bowl*, Vidal admires the later "James [who] is now giving us monsters on a divine scale" (182). Vidal suggests that James's literary efflorescence stems, in part, from the domestic pleasures associated most closely with romance, as James found himself comfortably installed in a new house and fell in love with a young man.

Vidal's self-alignment with James should not be understood only as a pining for a high literary mode. For one thing, this is not the basis on which he appreciates a "gay" James. For another, Vidal repeatedly exempts James from the fantasy, expressed in gendered terms by Schuyler and Hawthorne, that print ever offered independence from the market. Vidal may wish that his own literary stature were elevated to the level of James's, but this wish does not ground Vidal's successful management of literary fame in the age of TV, except insofar as Vidal recognizes that James also perceived the continuities between romance and novelistic achievement. One place this perception manifests itself in Vidal's work is in the similarities of voice shared by the lady romancer–cum–screenwriter Elinor Glyn in *Hollywood* and Myra Breckinridge. The casting of Joanna Lumley (of *Absolutely Fabulous* fame) as Elinor Glyn in Peter Bogdanovich's recent film *The Cat's Meow* (2001) would seem cognizant of the Myra tendencies of the Glyn character.

Encountering Glyn, a successful romance writer who wants to write a vehicle for Emma Traxler, Caroline "nearly curtsies" before

> the robust woman, swathed, like a sofa, in a purple velvet cloak that somewhat muted the turbulent masses of a glorious red wig that had been parted down the middle of an ursine head out of which peered the intelligent features of a green-eyed Irish girl, somewhat long in the tooth. (*Hollywood*, 270)

Readers of *Myra* will hear the overtones of that unforgettable voice in Elinor's "high priestess flow":

> "I would so much like to *create* for you. You are that rare thing, a woman of a certain age, but with allure. What I call, for want of a richer, more specific — for obvious reasons — word, 'it'!" "It." Caroline offered Miss Glyn her Madonna smile. "I would have thought that only women of childbearing age could have 'it.'" "It is not a reference to menstrual flow." "Nay," [Elinor continues] as if the word were in everyday use and not a blossom plucked from the pages of a vivid fiction, "even a woman of my

essential substance, willful, commanding, yes, in appearance and, perhaps, oh, the tiniest bit in real life, can still, when the moon shimmers in the sky and there is a scent of orange blossom upon the air, cause a dashing young Romeo to fall to his knees in an ecstasy of desire . . ."
"The position, I hope, is only temporary . . ." [Caroline interjects.] "Romeo must *start* on his knees. The rest depends on — Kismet." (271)

Although the dialogue manifests the differences in Glyn's and Caroline's levels of intelligence, the plot of the novel moves Caroline into closer proximity to Glyn as she adopts a Hollywood career. To see Elinor Glyn as an intermediary between the Jamesian Caroline and Myra Breckinridge is also to see the continuum that Vidal creates between romance, historical, and experimental writing, there both at the level of plot and at the level of source (in, e.g., the use of James alongside Anger).

Caroline's adulterous romance with the politician James Burden Day — begun in *Empire* and sustained, though it is ultimately broken off, in *Hollywood* — illustrates the continuum between romance and history in Vidal's writings. Vidal's Senator Burden Day offers Caroline access to the political back rooms of Washington, and she uses the information that he provides to further her newspaper career in many ways. Most salient, for Vidal's development of the back room–bedroom connections as well as for the problems that Caroline's status as a woman pose to her professional advancement, is her orchestrating his seduction of her half brother,

Blaise, which provides her with the leverage to blackmail Blaise into selling her his shares of the *Washington Tribune*. Placated by her revelation that he is actually the father of her child, Burden Day takes on the assignment, telling her: "It's the least I could do, for you giving me Emma."[5]

It is curious to note that Vidal names the initiator of one of the only scenes of homosexual sex in the American Chronicles after Jim Burden, the narrator of Willa Cather's *My Ántonia* (1918). In the triangulation between Caroline, James Burden Day, and Blaise, Vidal offers a view of homosexual behavior, here presented as engineered by Caroline in a politically moti- vated drama of incestuous revenge. The invocation of Cather, however, also suggests that Caroline's reproductive hetero- sexuality does not sanitize the opportunistic homosexuality; rather, it invites the recognition that Caroline, Cather's Bur- den's opposite number, serves Vidal, not only as a vehicle for male-male desire (a standard homosocial scenario), but also as a site through which male-identified male desire operates. As a male-identified career woman whose greatest sexual sat- isfaction is achieved through the manipulation of her lover into bed with her brother, Caroline is closer, perhaps, to Myra Breckinridge than one might otherwise suspect.[6]

Vidal's treatment in *The Golden Age* of Caroline — who is no less glamorous for having retired from the movie business, al- though now, in her seventies, somewhat less in control of the impression that her face-lifted face has on those around her — suggests the extent to which his Jamesian young lady has, with age and experience in Hollywood, come more closely to re- semble Myra. Now a spy for France whose mission is to persuade Roosevelt to enter World War II, Caroline characteristically worries about the impression that her appearance makes on others in the vocabulary of sets, lighting, sound track, and camera position. Moreover, she frequently holds her familiarity with European culture and history over the heads of the Washington politicos with whom she interacts, telling the hostess and newspaperwoman Cissy Patterson not to worry about the color clash between her stud's burgundy silk pajamas, which he sports under his clothes, with the peach of her bedroom decor because that was the color scheme of Mme du Deffand. When Cissy reveals her ignorance, responding, "I don't know her," Caroline, and Vidal, tactfully omit to mention that Mme du Deffand, whose famous salon was frequented by Voltaire and company, was blind.

The historical novels of Cather, Mary Renault, Marguerite Yourcenar, and Pat Barker, which use complicated identifications across gender and across sexualities, provide a literary context for Vidal's writing across these lines from the opposite direction. Like Vidal, Barker, Renault, and Yourcenar make visible powerful currents of desire that include historical desire; that is, they situate desire in history even as they evince a desire *for* history.[7] This desire does not turn history into any more of an explanation or a cause than it is postmodernist historical fiction. Indeed, it remains unclear whether the leveling of fiction and history in postmodernist historical fiction, which subjects both texts of history and forms of narrative to the same processes of fragmentation and disjointment, actually represents a new conception of history, whether it makes history work differently than it does in the more conventional examples of historical romance. If writing romance permits Vidal to situate his fictional achievement alongside that of his canonical predecessors, it also structures the way in which he situates his work in relation to that of his bestselling contemporaries.

Bestsellers

It is often difficult to distinguish the notes of high-minded disdain from the tones of sardonic glee in Vidal's writing, especially when he discusses the novel and the advent of the newer technologies. It is worth bearing in mind that the man who would miss no opportunity to have sex or appear on TV has published numerous bestsellers, including *Julian, Washington, D.C., Myra Breckinridge, Burr, 1876,* and *Lincoln.* He has also published a number of genre novels, including one romance, *A Star's Progress* (1950), under the pseudonym Katherine Everard (the surname taken from the famous Everard Baths), and the three murder mysteries *Death in the Fifth Position, Death before Bedtime,* and *Death Likes It Hot* published between 1952 and 1954 under a pseudonym that suggests the television, Edgar Box.[8] These incursions into pulp, lucrative considering the time invested (*A Star's Progress* earned him $1,000 for one week's work [Kaplan, *Gore Vidal,* 316]), provided Vidal with an insight into the intersections of romance, politics, and history key to his later endeavors.

Death before Bedtime, the middle of the Box trilogy, for example, is narrated by Peter Sargeant, a journalist turned detective, and features his adventures at the Washington home of Senator Rhodes, whose murder catalyzes the plot. Ellen Rhodes, the alcoholic, nymphomaniac daughter of the senator, closely resembles Enid Sanford Overbury, the self-destructive daughter of Blaise Sanford whose marriage to the presidential hopeful Clay Overbury makes up much of the plot of *Washington, D.C.* As Kaplan notes, Enid Sanford's promiscuous escapades owe a great deal to those of Vidal's mother, Nina Gore Auchincloss (*Gore Vidal*, 571). *Death before Bedtime* opens with a sex scene between Peter Sargeant and Ellen Rhodes. Sex between the first-person narrator and a character who resembles the author's mother suggests that pseudonymously published genre fiction supplies a dry run for an oedipal fantasy, rewritten in a serious novel as a family romance. As Vidal states in the autobiographical *Screening History*, he centered the narrative of *Washington, D.C.* on the two houses in which he grew up—that of his grandfather, Senator Gore of Oklahoma, at Rock Creek Park and that of his stepfather, Hugh Auchincloss, on the south bank of the Potomac in McLean, Virginia, known as Merrywood. His description continues:

> I was there and not there in the text. I had revealed and not revealed my peculiar family. I had also, without intending to, started on a history of the American republic as experienced by one family and its emblematic connection to Aaron Burr. During the next quarter-century I re-dreamed the republic's history, which I have always regarded as a family affair. (11)

In *Washington, D.C.*, both terms, family and romance, are projected outward, and their significance is rendered in terms of American political history. The germ of the American Chronicles that extends these insights backward two centuries could thus be said to be romance.

A Star's Progress, set mainly in the early 1940s, charts the rise of a young girl, Grace Carter, originally Graziella Serrano from Monterrey, Mexico, through the seedy world of Bourbon Street burlesque clubs, to Hollywood stardom. True to romance conventions, the temporal and geographic specifics through which Grace moves are conjured by only the merest of gestures. However, Vidal allows history to disrupt the conventions of romance at two significant points in the novel, signaling the relations between romance and history as they take shape in the historical fiction of Vidal's American Chronicles. The second of these two prominent intrusions happens near the end of the novel, marking its climax. The outbreak of war makes it impossible for Frederick, the crown prince of a Balkan country that remains nameless, to continue his affair with Grace, who has fallen in love for the first time. The novel thus resolves itself around Grace's mounting unhappiness as she realizes that, despite having fulfilled her dreams of fame and fortune, she will never find satisfaction in love.

The first intrusion happens in the first paragraph of the novel and signals that the outcome of the novel's plot will hinge on the impact of such historical events on the lives of its characters, who aspire to live outside history. *A Star's Progress* opens:

The gray-pink city of Monterrey was quiet. It was early Sunday evening and people were returning from a carnival on the outskirts of town. In the central plaza of the city, which enclosed dark green trees and a fountain, men and women sat side by side; some few strolled about, circling the plaza slowly—half going in one direction, half in the other. Electric lights cast a pale yellow reflection across the town, for there was not much electric power during the second decade of the twentieth century which would, though none knew it, reshape not only Monterrey and Mexico, but the entire world.[9]

Portentous, resoundingly off-key, and, moreover, completely irrelevant to the plot, this description of the impact of electricity is, nevertheless, perfectly in keeping with Vidal's sense of the importance of history, more specifically, the history of technology, to narrative.

Vidal himself suggests the context of the bestsellers for understanding his success in America in the interview given to *Gay Sunshine* magazine in 1974. When asked, "How does it strike you that *Myron* will not reach a large audience?" Vidal replies: "I always have to remind myself that I'm in America, and that I'm the author of a bad, dirty book like Jacqueline Susann or Harold Robbins."[10] Although Vidal here appears as the suave expatriate, sneering at both American puritanism and bad literary judgment, it is worth taking up the invitation to consider him in this company, for Susann's *The Valley of the Dolls* (1966) and *The Love Machine* and Robbins's *The Carpetbaggers* (1961) share Vidal's concern with the eclipse of print cultures by screen cultures that accompanies the westward shift of American cultural production from New York to Los Angeles.

Despite sharing with him both subject matter and desired audience, however, Vidal goes out of his way to differentiate himself as a writer from Harold Robbins and everything he represents in a review of the "Top Ten Best-Sellers of January, 1973." This essay assesses the merits of the books under consideration in terms of the films that their writers have unintentionally translated (or failed to translate) into print. Vidal dismisses Robbins in scathing terms: he is too primitive a writer to imagine "anything exciting to add to what the reader has already learned from gossip columns and magazine interviews" (*United States*, 72) in his treatment of the golden dozen of Hollywood legend. Robbins lacks the requisite skills to integrate history and fiction, skills at which Vidal excels. Indeed, at stake in this review is the status of bestsellerdom, and Vidal presents himself as chastened by its market mechanisms under the tutelage of the Wise Hack, who proclaims in the review's first words: "Shit has its own integrity" (67). Cleverly positioning himself, not as a bestselling novelist, but as a writer who has paid his dues in Hollywood, he conducts this survey from the writers' table at the studio commissary. Vidal thus vests his authority in a firsthand experience of the production end of screen culture, but his suggestion that writing for film and television supplants literary expertise is complicated by his satirical conclusion. Suspecting that the Wise Hack will long be honored and remembered for his contributions, Vidal places himself "humbly below the salt," alongside writers of more secure canonical stature—Isherwood, Faulkner, and Huxley. Collectively, they have mistakenly "preferred perversely to write books that reflected not the movies we had seen but life itself"; "none of us regarded with sufficient seriousness the greatest art form of all time" (88).

We should not let this blatant sarcasm override the affection for the movies evident in the lovingly detailed evocation of their presence in the bestsellers that Vidal discusses. *Screening History* extends this treatment of Hollywood with considerably more fondness. It is also noteworthy that Vidal introduced the concluding paragraph of "Top Ten Best-Sellers" by likening the state of mind induced by reading those books to being trapped in the Late-Late Show, the premise of *Myron*, which was probably being composed around the same time.

Although Vidal went out of his way to attack Robbins, he remained silent about the other person into whose company he put himself in the *Gay Sunshine* interview: Jacqueline Susann. The comparison may seem unlikely at first glance. Susann herself noted in her comments to Berney Geis, the publisher of *The Valley of the Dolls*, on turning in her third rewrite: "The day is over when the point of writing is to turn a phrase that critics will quote, like Henry James. I'm not interested in turning a phrase."[11] Her clunky writing is an equally far cry from both James's masterful prose and the elegant sentences in which Vidal dresses up his historical materials. However, like Vidal, not only did Susann enjoy celebrity

10. Jacqueline Susann on the set of *The Love Machine*.
Courtesy of Photofest.

status, but her writing about it also cast light on the place of the writer in the age of TV (figure 10).

The framing device of one of the bestselling novels of all times, *The Valley of the Dolls*—that anatomy of the double bind of female celebrity—consists of the romance between Anne Welles, the classy girl from New England, and Lyon Burke, the failed writer. Even as celebrity drives the other characters west from New York to Los Angeles, Lyon, who has returned from the battlefields of World War II with a newly awakened literary ambition, moves "back" from New York to England to follow, with Anne's encouragement, his noble artistic pursuit. Lyon's conviction that the ability to write aesthetically important fiction is contingent on being located away from the centers of Broadway, film, and TV production, ideally with the emotional support of a financially dependent domesticated wife, is in striking contrast to Susann's own pursuit of success, first on Broadway, then as a television star, then as a writer who typed her manuscript drafts on color-coded paper in the New York hotel room that served as her apartment. Lyon's nostalgia for the romantic artist is not Susann's. Not only does his failure to sustain such a practice serve to underline her own bestselling success; it also suggests a gendered critique of the romantic artist as a male prerogative.

Like Vidal, Susann also had firsthand experience of TV. Between 1955 and 1959, she had been the spokesperson for Schiffli, a machine process for making lace and embroidery. A group of manufacturers who used this process sponsored the TV programs on which Susann appeared as host. She also wrote and presented the Schiffli spots that were aired regularly between 1955 and 1959 on other programs as well, including, at least occasionally, David Susskind's *Open End* on Channel 13, the show that Vidal guest-hosted briefly in 1963.

On the occasion of the publication of *The Love Machine*, Susann appeared as a guest on *The David Frost Show* (July 16, 1969; figure 11). During the fifteen-minute one-on-one interview, Frost asked her to place herself among contemporary authors such as Norman Mailer and Phillip Roth. Susann deftly deflected the question by saying: "It would be like asking you, 'Are you like Merv Griffin?' when you are unique." The next segment of the program pitted her, sitting at the foot of the stage, against three critics, seated in the audience: Rex Reed, Nora Ephron, and John Simon. Asked to discuss the

11. David Frost on the set of his show.
Courtesy of Photofest.

phenomenal appeal of Susann's novels, Ephron talked about
the female pleasures of reading romance, which turned into
a defense of Susann when John Simon went on the rampage,
declaring that Susann was not a writer but a showbiz tycoon.
Susann displayed her characteristic telegenic wit developed
when she was a host on the first all-night local TV show, *Night
Time, New York* (1955), and on *Night Beat* (1956), the confrontational interview show that launched Mike Wallace's career,
by turning to the audience. They responded by booing and

hissing Simon's defense of the canon of high literature and wildly applauding Susann's invitations to laugh at Simon's expense. She poked fun at his professorial demeanor and his Eastern European accent, and then he sputtered about his academic qualifications (as a Yale PH.D. in comparative literature) and, gesticulating in frustration, exclaimed: "But she's not Flaubert!" Indeed, contra Simon, whom he skewered in "Literary Gangsters" (1970), Vidal links academic literary study to the kind of illiteracy that others associate with TV.

Susann helped revolutionize the ways in which books were marketed with her use of television, celebrity tie-ins, and promotional paraphernalia. In "Wasn't She Great?" a piece originally published in the *New Yorker*, later adapted for the biopic about Susann entitled *Isn't She Great?* (directed by Andrew Bergman, 2000), Michael Korda appreciated Susann's lesson "that books can be merchandised, just like anything else—something that a lot of publishers have yet to learn."[12] But, more than the marketing know-how that she bequeathed to the book industry, Susann's success also seems to have represented a demasculinization of American literary culture to Vidal's more macho literary contemporaries, including Norman Mailer and Saul Bellow. The new form of bestsellerdom spearheaded by Susann prompted Vidal to produce a set of discriminations for the assessment of this writing, as the comparison between bestselling novels and films in "Top Ten Best-Sellers" shows.

Robin Stone, the hero of *The Love Machine* and Susann's personification of the love machine, makes perfectly explicit the relations between love and television. He says: "Let's talk about television. It's no longer just a little box, it's the Love Machine. Because it sells love. It creates love. It's turned politicians into movie stars and movie stars into politicians. It's the pulse and heart of the twentieth century— the Love Machine."[13] Susann called herself a "natural on the boob-tube";[14] Myra Breckinridge, the boob tube incarnate, is Susann's unnatural counterpart. Vidal's public appeal, which has included periodic appearances *as* Myra, rests on his ability to telecast and write out of a position that does not cordon off serious literature from a mass audience: rather, it brings Henry James and Jacqueline Susann together.

When Vidal put himself into Susann's company in the *Gay Sunshine* interview, he performed a campy publicity stunt that may well have been inspired by her. If not, then at least it could be said that both learned such tricks in the same place—in the entertainment world of 1950s New York. Much of Susann's wit derives from the milieu of the Jewish comics, including Jerry Lewis, around Broadway in the 1940s, a sensibility too vaudeville and too ethnic for Vidal, one that stands in strong contrast with his Washington-bred patrician demeanor, which he uses to effect the cool, incisive wit of an outsider who, though the ultimate WASP, stands alone, with no party, no family, and no partner. But, like Susann, Jerry Lewis has much in common with Vidal's Myra. I put Vidal in the company of Susann (just as I put him in the company of Jerry Lewis earlier) in order to suggest an alternative genealogy for the intellectual, one excluded from those accounts that have been dominated by the print-based model of the intellectual. If Vidal maintains the status of exemplary American writer-intellectual in the age of TV, it is because he has both exploited the print-screen circuit in the genre of romance and found ways to transmit his sexual politics on-screen.

n 1948, Vidal published *The City and the Pillar*, the first explicit treatment of homosexuality in American fiction. He subsequently revised the novel in 1965 and wrote a new preface when it was republished for a British edition in 1995.[1] The 1965 revisions display his adherence to a universalizing understanding of homosexuality, one that posits a bisexual disposition for most people and resists the notion that special identities follow from sexual behavior. In the 1995 preface, Vidal rearticulated this position for the decade of queer theory and activism, but he framed the novel with an account of his election of a literary over a political career.

A Literary or a Political Career

Vidal thoroughly rewrote *The City and the Pillar* for style in 1965 in order to rid his prose of its late-1940s Farrellesque flatness. The single most significant change that he made was to the novel's climax. In the 1948 version, Jim Willard, the hero, resumes contact with Bob Ford, his boyhood friend and lover now recently married, makes a sexual overture after a drunken evening, is rebuffed — and kills Bob. In the 1965 version, Vidal has Jim rape rather than kill Bob.

The 1965 edition includes a preface, "The City and the Pillar after Twenty Years," in which Vidal reflected on the revisions. Having broken the mold and challenged how male lovers were represented, he was, he said, dissatisfied with the book's ending:

> The coda was unsatisfactory. At the time it was generally believed that the publishers forced me to tack on a cautionary ending in much the same way as the Motion Picture Code insists that wickedness be punished. This was not true. I had always meant the end of the book to be black, but not as black as it turned out. (48)

Vidal cast his alteration of the novel's ending in terms of a contrast between his relative freedom as an author and the constraints of Hayes Code–governed cinematic production. The comparison between page and screen here emphasizes their differences rather than their similarities, but, as in *Myra Breckinridge*, *Myron*, *Duluth*, and *Live from Golgotha*, the print-screen circuit becomes a vehicle through which Vidal conveys his sexual politics. Revisiting the moment in which he, at twenty-two, published his third novel, first from the vantage point of twenty years later, and then again from that of fifty years later, Vidal also offers a synoptic view of changes in the cultural and political status of homosexuality.

In the 1965 preface, Vidal described his literary goals,

specifying his desire to "do something risky, that no American had done before":

> I decided to examine the homosexual underworld (which I knew rather less well than I pretended), and in the process show the naturalness of homosexual relations, as well as making the point that there is of course no such thing as a homosexual. (*City and Pillar*, 45)

This apparent paradox—of establishing at one and the same time the naturalness of homosexuality and the nonexistence of the homosexual—is one that Vidal has frequently repeated.

For Vidal, there is no such thing as a homosexual because the word is not a noun; it is an adjective that describes sex acts. "Sex is," as he put it in a 1960 review of Mailer's *Advertisements for Myself* (1959). "No other meanings follow, and as a result, attempts to make them follow are simply wrongheaded" (*United States*, 37). Yet, in his depiction in the 1965 preface of what the novel initially achieved, he emphasized the political repercussions of his representation of homosexuality, an emphasis that stands in tension with his claim that "sex [merely] is."

Vidal has reprinted "Sex and the Law" (1965) with later editions of *The City and the Pillar*. According to the introduction he added to the Andre Deutsch edition, the novel contributed to the changes in Australia's obscenity laws because when *The City and the Pillar* was confiscated and brought to trial, the judge acknowledged he thought the case absurd. Though Vidal may indeed have had a hand in altering Australian obscenity laws, here he conflated *The City and the Pillar* with *Myra Breckinridge*, the novel that was confiscated from Dennis Altman, political scientist and gay rights activist, in 1969. Judge Levine found against the book, though Australian anti-pornography laws were subsequently changed. By recounting this partly invented reception of *The City and the Pillar*, Vidal invited readers to situate the novel in some relation to his more explicitly political statements about sex even though he also took pains to disavow the idea that anything follows, politically or aesthetically, from sexual practices.

When he reflected in the 1995 preface on the alterations

that he made to *The City and the Pillar*, Vidal once again revisited the relations among literature, sexuality, and politics. He presented himself on the eve of the novel's first publication as at a crossroads: his grandfather, Senator Gore of Oklahoma, was arranging a political career for him in New Mexico at the time he wrote *The City and the Pillar*, but "honor requir[ed] the publication of the novel," and the career in politics was sacrificed. Although he "wanted very much to be a politician, nature had designed [him] to be a writer" (2). A complicated analogy, in which Vidal described himself, like Oedipus, at the fork dividing the roads to Athens and Thebes, suggests that choosing literature was, for him, a form of parricide (Oedipus kills his father at that fork). The oedipal scenario has since Freud been taken as central to the acquisition of sexual identity, but Vidal here suspends the sexual resonance and mobilizes that famous scene to characterize his acquisition of a writerly career, which, he suggests, was permanent.

It is curious, then, that nowhere in either preface did Vidal acknowledge that, in 1960, he pursued a congressional campaign and that, in 1982, he ran for Senate. In other words, he retrospectively claimed that, in 1948, he understood publishing a gay novel to be career suicide for those aspiring to hold office, at least in New Mexico, even though it seems to have had this effect on him neither in New York State in 1960 nor in California in 1982. Furthermore, if Vidal saw homosexuality as having compromised his political ambitions in 1948, he didn't say so until 1995. In 1995, he depicted the 1948 choice of a literary over a political career as flowing from his desire to be a writer (with all the cultural prestige then associated with this position), not as a means to practice politics by other means. As the 1999 publication of his collected sex writings in the volume called *Sexually Speaking* attests, Vidal has exploited the public interest in the topic of sexuality and the political or cultural status that sexual orientation has come to have, even though he would suspend the connections between sexual practice and any particular political or aesthetic meanings.

In his treatment of Vidal's recent writings, Christopher Hitchens suggested that it may have irked Vidal more than he let on to have missed the opportunity to be elected to public office, yet Vidal himself has never said as much, apparently ready to accept the vicissitudes of the democratic process.[2] The 1995 autobiographical preface suggests that writing a gay novel forced a choice between culture and politics. But other writings reveal Vidal refusing to treat culture and politics as competing alternatives. It turns out that, for Vidal, sexuality trips the circuit on which culture and politics sit.

In what may be Vidal's most abstract treatment of power, the early essay "The Twelve Caesars" (written in 1952, published in *The Nation* in 1959), prompted by the appearance of Robert Graves's translation of Suetonius, sexuality turns out to be key. That essay concludes: "In holding up a mirror to those Caesars of diverting legend, [Suetonius] reflects not only on them but ourselves: half-tamed creatures, whose great moral task is to hold in balance the angel and the monster within— for we are both and to ignore this duality is to invite disaster" (*United States*, 528).[3] As such a resounding conclusion suggests, Vidal seeks to show the perpetual corrupting force of absolute power. In order to establish the connections between the past and the present, he must display the differences, which he does in the first half of the essay by comparing classical and modern conceptions of sexual norms. He lays out the differences between "us," for whom "the norm is heterosexual; the family is central; all else is deviation, pleasing or not depending on one's own tastes and moral preoccupations" (525), and the classics, for whom man is assumed to be various. In a signature gesture, Vidal effects the transition from sexuality to power by ruminating on the caesars as writers. He then bridges the presumed gap between sexuality and power and between the classics and ourselves:

> One suspects that despite the stern moral legislation of our own time other human beings are no different. If nothing else, Dr. Kinsey revealed in his dogged, arith-

metical way that we are all less predictable and bland than anyone had suspected. (525)

Sexual Behavior in the Human Male (1948), Kinsey's powerful intervention into the categorization of homosexuality as a "third sex," insisted that homosexuality be defined as a type of sex act, not as a type of person. As Kinsey asserted:

> It would encourage clearer thinking on these matters if persons were not characterized as heterosexual or homosexual, but as individuals who have had certain amounts of heterosexual experience and certain amounts of homosexual experience. Instead of using these terms as substantives which stand for persons, or even as adjectives to describe persons, they may be better used to describe the nature of overt sexual relations, or of the stimuli to which an individual erotically responds.[4]

Although much controversy, summarized in two recent biographies, has called into question the methods that Kinsey used to collect his data—which established that one in three men had at some point in life had at least one homosexual encounter leading to orgasm—his work continues to be hailed as a significant contribution to the scientific study of sexuality, and his findings enabled the striking of homosexuality from the lists of mental illness in 1973. Vidal happily includes in the 1965 preface to *The City and the Pillar* Kinsey's note thanking Vidal for "your work in the field" (47). Indeed, the congruence between Vidal's and Kinsey's treatments of homosexuality is complete.

In her groundbreaking *Epistemology of the Closet*, Eve Kosofsky Sedgwick proposes a useful distinction between universalizing and minoritizing understandings of homosexuality. In the universalizing understanding, questions of sexual definition matter for everyone, whereas, in the minoritizing understanding, they matter for a few.[5] Vidal embraces a universalizing understanding of homosexuality. He also believes that the idea that sexual orientation constitutes an identity is a mistake. He has repeatedly denied that there is such a thing as a homosexual, that the term *homosexual* is not a noun. The correct view, according to him, is that most people are capable of, may desire, and may also have experienced homosexual sex acts, that there is a universal capacity for homosexual behavior. In the parlance of current queer theory, Vidal adheres to an acts-based rather than identity-based understanding of sexuality. He insists that most people, among whom he includes himself, are bisexually oriented. For Vidal, sexuality is of universal concern, though it is not possible to generalize any political or cultural consequences from this fact. Interestingly, this understanding has not minimized his attention to matters of sexuality. Rather, his awareness that sex can be mobilized for varying political effects has made him an alert commentator on the ways in which it has been used.

In the hilarious 1970 essay "Doc Reuben," for example, Vidal attacked the failure of those who would embrace sexual liberation to acknowledge that bisexuality exists, even going so far as to signal his own bisexuality:

Dr. Reubens [*sic*] cannot accept the following simple fact of so many lives (certainly my own): that it is possible to have a mature sexual relationship with a woman on Monday, and a mature sexual relationship with a man on Tuesday, and perhaps on Wednesday have both together (admittedly you have to be in good condition for this). (*United States*, 581)

Vidal has made no secret of his homosexual experiences. They have had a curious impact on his political ambitions — and not the one we might expect. Although he represented the publication of *The City and the Pillar* as a crossroads in his career when he elected literature rather than politics, neither of his two subsequent campaigns for public office seem to have been impeded by questions about his sexual orientation. It is interesting to consider the extent to which Vidal's understanding of sexuality allowed him to slip beneath the radar of American homophobic political culture.

Vidal vs. Buckley

The public invisibility of Vidal's sexual orientation ended, however, in August 1968, when he was outed on national TV by the ultraconservative talking head William F. Buckley Jr., with whom he covered the Democratic national convention for ABC (figures 12 and 13). As students and riot police clashed outside the convention hall in downtown Chicago, Buckley and Vidal nearly came to blows in an episode that was said to have rocked television. When Vidal criticized Buckley's support of Mayor Daley's use of force to quash the protestors, calling him a "pro- or crypto-Nazi," Buckley yelled: "Now listen, you queer. Stop calling me a pro crypto Nazi or I'll sock you in the goddamn face and you'll stay plastered. . . ." ABC bleeped Buckley's words in its West Coast broadcast.

Both Buckley and Vidal were invited to give their sides of the story to *Esquire* magazine,[6] but lengthy lawsuits followed the appearance of Vidal's essay, Buckley suing both Vidal and *Esquire* for libel, and Vidal countersuing Buckley. Vidal's biographer, Fred Kaplan, does a fine job with the intricacies of the protracted print and legal conflicts, pointing out that public perception gave the victory to Vidal, not

12. William F. Buckley Jr. wraps himself in the flag. Courtesy of Photofest.

13. Vidal in 1968.
Courtesy of Photofest.

necessarily because he had done any more effective a job
at conveying his political beliefs than had Buckley, but because Buckley had basically lost control of himself, an em-
barrassment increased by his betrayal of one of his own prin-
ciples, that there is no place for bad language, a form of
immorality, in political debate. Though Vidal was clearly in-
flammatory himself, *Nazi* was a recognizable political term
in 1968, while *queer* was not—it was private, as ABC's bleep-
ing decision registers. Moreover, in the decisions made by the
courts around Buckley's libel suit against Vidal, which in all
likelihood prompted Buckley to drop the charges, the judge
found admissible articles that Buckley had written for the *National Review*. The anti-Semitism, racism, and other identi-
fiable strands of fascism evident in Buckley's writing would
have made it possible for Vidal's lawyers to defend his behavior on the basis of both "heat of debate" and "fair comment"
(*Gore Vidal*, 615). In Vidal's *Esquire* piece, he had staged his

14. The Buckley
clan on the cover
of *Life* magazine.
William F. Buckley Jr.
seated in center
with dog. Courtesy
of Photofest.

justification for having called Buckley a "pro- or crypto-Nazi"
around the revelation that, in 1944, Buckley's sisters had
been tried for and found guilty of vandalizing an Episcopal
church in Sharon, Connecticut, whose minister's wife was the
real estate agent who had sold a house in the neighborhood
to a Jewish family (figure 14).

Curiously, Buckley has continued to wage this battle with
both Vidal and *Esquire*. The December 31, 2004, issue of
the *National Review* reported a legal settlement that Buckley sought when *Esquire* included Vidal's "Distasteful Encounter" in *Esquire's Big Book of Great Writing*:[7] *Esquire* had
to supply Buckley's essay "On Experiencing Gore Vidal" to
readers who requested it and to post it on its website for the
two months beginning February 15, 2005. Buckley grasped

an opportunity to gain public attention spawned by the forgetfulness of *Esquire*'s editors, who reprinted an essay that had been subject to litigation. Forcing *Esquire* to withdraw this collection, Buckley exploited the slender possibility that he would come to be regarded as the victor even though he never won the initial litigation. Indeed, one could take the inclusion of Vidal's essay in the collection as Vidal's vindication. Perhaps the most salient aspect of this ongoing saga is its validation of Vidal's accounts of American amnesia.

Initially, Vidal had been willing—before Buckley took the scandal to the pages of *Esquire*—to dismiss the kerfuffle, getting his own back again when he told the *Chicago Sun-Times* in a morning-after interview: "I've always tried to treat Buckley like the great lady that he is. He's given to neurotic tantrums and I feel sorry for him" (cited in Kaplan, *Gore Vidal*, 604). If, in this comment, Vidal capitalizes on Buckley's introduction of the sexual into the political domain to use the "it takes one to know one" retort, it is equally clear that he was prepared to consign the exchange of sexual attributions to a para-public domain and to let the matter drop.

The thrust of Buckley's *Esquire* piece is that Vidal's sexual preferences make him immoral. According to Buckley, Vidal sets out to show that homosexuality is superior to heterosexuality; his fiction, one vehicle through which he ostensibly makes this argument, is pornographic; and it thus follows that Vidal's political opinions are suspect. Vidal evaded Buckley's provocation to take up the relations between sexuality and politics in the register of identity because he conceived them differently.

The legacy of 1968 was the topic of a series of seminars put on by the Museum of Broadcasting in New York City in 1988. One panel, specifically devoted to exploring the impact of 1968 on television, featured speakers such as Bill Leonard, the former president of CBS, Robert Northshield, the former NBC elections producer and executive producer at CBS, Dan Rather, Mike Wallace, a number of other television bigwigs, and one non-TV person, Senator Eugene McCarthy. The videotaped record of this event, archived in the New York branch of the Museum of TV and Radio, contains a surprising revelation: the panelists agree that, of all the world-altering events of that tumultuous year, which included the assassinations of Martin Luther King and Robert Kennedy, May in Paris, and the Soviet invasion of Czechoslovakia, the most significant, as far as television was concerned, was the Democratic convention in Chicago. Only McCarthy dissents, insisting that the most significant event of that year was the escalation of the war in Vietnam, but the TV people keep to topic, describing the Democratic convention as itself a war, one that, in Bill Leonard's words, was "perpetrated by Mayor Daley" and "the television and media people lost." It is their view, then, that the Democratic convention constituted a trauma for TV.

The panelists' reminiscences of overcoming the technical challenges posed by Mayor Daley's media blackout are overshadowed by their recollections of the response of affiliates, sponsors, and executive higher-ups, including the FCC, which, in the aftermath of the riots, rebuked news producers for having inappropriately taken the side of the demonstrators.

According to Leonard, in the aftermath of Chicago, the TV people were subjected to the worst pressures in the history of the medium, ones that reshaped their relations to the networks as well as TV's relation to the public in general. North-shield, who had developed the Huntley-Brinkley show for NBC but had moved to PBS around this time, reveals that antiwar sentiment was more actively censored on public TV than on the other networks. He is most succinct about the results of this episode: after Chicago, it was no longer possible to view TV, or for TV to view itself, as an observer of events; TV had become a participant. The shock of the TV producers at finding themselves implicated in events toward which they had hitherto believed themselves neutral is the flip side of the demonstrators' co-optation of TV to shame the police out of their brutalizing behavior with their rallying cry: "The whole world is watching." Even if student protestors and TV people had different political goals, taken together their responses register the then-new recognition of the personal as the political, the slogan of identity politics.

Buckley's use of print and TV to out Vidal shares with the TV people, who saw Chicago 1968 as a turning point in TV's mode of functioning, the view that TV, as a participant in politics, is a vehicle for identity. By contrast, Vidal uses TV in the political essays on sex and, especially, in *Myra Breckinridge* and its sequel, *Myron*, to practice a sexual politics that does not turn on identity. It is through the print-screen circuit that Vidal has conveyed most effectively his universalizing acts-based conception of sexuality.

In an interview that he gave to the *New Left Review* in 1985, Vidal describes his experiences writing *The City and the Pillar* as what radicalized him:

> Where is the radicalization, if it can be so called? I think it started with seeing the way in which the country tried to exclude anybody who was critical of its precepts: in this case, of its sexual politics. I don't think I had formulated very much at that time, but I thought that this was really a rather ugly society, that I had become a nonwriter on sectarian grounds; it was just what would happen in the Soviet Union.

In Vidal's retrospective account, radicalization occurred when he became aware that sexual (like literary) preferences could exclude him from the political arena. Yet he proceeds to tell the *New Left* interviewer: "I went into television drama. During that time the blacklisting began and all my friends were victims of it. I was too young to have been a Communist. Here I was with considerable power in television. Then there was McCarthyism." The grandson of the conservative populist Senator Gore of Oklahoma, and the son of a "very, very conservative" West Pointer, Vidal thus "had an immaculate right-wing background. I was perfectly clean." He was in the ideal position to write subversive TV drama, which he did in *A Sense of Justice* (ca. 1953). Significantly, Vidal gives equal play to TV as a source of his radicalization. He concludes:

"Television helped me to develop as a writer, as well as giving me a lesson in how the country works."[8]

In the 1995 preface to *The City and the Pillar*, Vidal presented his political ambitions as having been blocked by his opting for literature (even though this was not the case), yet, in the 1985 *New Left* interview, he portrayed the switch from print to TV as having enabled him to sustain his political aims. Perhaps the sense that he was politically thwarted by the choice of a literary career conditioned his optimism throughout the 1960s about TV as a medium both for political subversion and through which writers broadened their access to the public. Even if this optimism later flagged, throughout his career TV has provided an ideal vehicle for Vidal's practice of sexual politics. In a sense, then, TV offered Vidal the vehicle with which to cross the gap between culture and politics in a nonidentitarian register.

In the 1979 essay "Sex Is Politics," Vidal put politics and sex into explicit relation to one another, and TV played a key role. Prescient about the ways in which the Moral Majority would come to articulate its platform of family values throughout the Reagan-Bush years, Vidal rightly located the backlash against the sexual revolution in a discussion of the "hot button" that sex had come to be in the domain of political discourse. Not only had sex become a major issue in that election year, but "the sexual attitudes of any given society are [always] the result of political decisions" (*Sexually Speaking*, 98). Vidal's analysis of sex is strictly political, concerned with the relations among religion and the state, election campaign financing, and the democratic process. The 1979 essay is also introduced by one of Vidal's signature gestures: a consideration of what it is and is not possible to say on TV.

" 'But surely you do not favor the publishing of pornography?' " The scene that Vidal sets is of a talk-show exchange, and the momentum that he builds for his argument has much to do with his reflections on how he has learned to effectively formulate and convey his positions in that medium. Significantly, however, the essay, published in *Playboy*, clearly offers Vidal a more congenial forum than did the box. Televisual discussion formats oblige him to utter, "Sex is politics," a phrase whose proper unpacking best occurs on the page: "Television is a great leveler. You always end up sounding like the people who ask the questions." Though Vidal "knows that [he] could never explain [him]self in the seven remaining in-depth minutes of air time" (*Sexually Speaking*, 97, 98), resorting, in the year or two since the television encounter, to print, he gets print mileage out of the media-savvy awareness of the time constraints of the TV-interview format ("seven remaining . . . minutes"), gleefully telling the reader that he was distracted, mentally rearranging the toupee of his interlocutor.

His perception that TV makes everyone sound the same moves Vidal to supplement his views in print. But, despite the complaint that TV levels communication, he casts the opportunities afforded by print in terms of a comparison to TV. He does not abandon TV in print; rather, he moves in print across the print-screen divide. Vidal's adaptation of his TV appearance to print expands the possibilities for democratic politics by using a televisual mode of address, even as he ruminates on what it is and is not possible to say on TV.

Vidal thus discovers an effective mode of address for conveying his political views to a televisual public, that is, a public conditioned by television even when its constituents peruse a book or magazine. His management of this political opportunity should be factored back into accounts of the intellectual. When Buckley called Vidal *queer* on the air, or when the panelists described the legacy of 1968 to TV as having transformed it from observer into participant, they show how TV can be used to practice identity politics. For Vidal, it offers the opposite opportunity: to practice sexual politics in a non-identitarian register.

Vidal's insistently universalizing treatments of sexuality have come to seem frustratingly idiosyncratic, especially to those, like the playwright and gay activist Larry Kramer, who would enlist Vidal for gay activism (see the interview with Kramer in *Sexually Speaking*). In his adherence to a universalizing understanding of homosexuality, Vidal refuses identity politics. Taking the television as a vehicle for this refusal, Vidal seeks the broadest audience that he can access. Traversing the print-screen divide, he passes up no opportunity to have sex or appear on TV. The goal may be pleasure, or it may be to achieve specific political aims, the critique of the Reagan-Bush family values platform in "Sex Is Politics," for example. The crossings are opportunistic, but they are also consistent insofar as they are motivated by the coherence of his political agenda. The televisual mode of address, on TV and in print, is their vehicle, but his sexual politics are also figured by television, both in and in relation to print. This convergence of sex and TV is most visible in his experimental fiction.

Vidal has always proposed that his fiction be divided into two types: the historical novels and the experimental novels, which he calls *inventions*. In the historical novels, film is for historical reasons the screen medium through which he explores the shift from print to screen modes of publicity. In the inventions, TV is the medium. TV affords Vidal the opportunity for great inventiveness, a use of the medium that counters narratives of its deadening effects. Vidal has also proved himself to be a powerful analyst of the organization of Hollywood in its post-1940s incarnation, the film/TV system, especially in *Myra Breckinridge*, *Myron*, and *Live from Golgotha*. In these novels, both sexuality and television lie at the heart of his accounts of the print-screen shift.

5 TV: Another Erogenous Zone

Public opinion exists only where there are no ideas.
Oscar Wilde, "A Few Maxims"

n 1968, Buckley used the appearance of *Myra Breckinridge* in print to smear Vidal as a pornographer. One could read Vidal's bestseller as a document of the 1960s sexual revolution, an ecstatic, utopian celebration of homosexuality and transsexuality that is secondarily concerned with the relations between print and film. To give the media only secondary status, however, would be a mistake. In the novel, and especially in its sequel, *Myron* (1974), Vidal is equally interested in print, film, and television and in the sexual opportunities provided by each. Indeed, Myra, Vidal's gorgeous transsexual heroine, is the boob tube incarnate. Dildo-wielding possessor of a pair of "once and future" beautiful breasts (*Myron*, 248), Myra is Vidal's linchpin between the page and both the screens, between romance and history.

Myra Breckinridge opens: "I am Myra Breckinridge whom no man will ever possess" (3). Animating herself through a series of similar pronouncements, Myra proclaims on the novel's next page,

> I am the New Woman whose astonishing history is a poignant amalgam of vulgar dreams and knife-sharp realities. Yet not even I can create a fictional character as one-dimensional as the average reader. Nevertheless, I intend to create a literary masterpiece in much the same way as I created myself, and for much the same reason: because it is not there. And I shall accomplish this by presenting you, the reader, with an exact, literal sense of what it is like to be me, what it is like to possess superbly shaped breasts reminiscent of those sported by Jean Harlow in *Hell's Angels* and seen at their best four minutes after the start of the second reel. What it is like to possess perfect thighs with hips resembling that archetypal mandolin from which the male principle draws forth music with prick of flesh so akin — in this simile — to prick of celluloid, *blessed* celluloid upon which have been imprinted in our century all our dreams and shadows that have haunted the human race since man's harsh and turbulent origins (quote Lévi-Strauss). Myra Breckinridge is a dish, and never forget it, you motherfuckers, as the children say nowadays. (4–5)

Myra's mission, "to re-create the sexes and thus save the human race from certain extinction" (6), is nominally directed toward Rusty and Mary-Ann, two students at Buck Loner's Academy of Drama and Modeling, whom she seduces into broadening their sexual horizons. In setting and tone, *Myra Breckinridge* has something in common with the contemporaneous porn satires of Russ Meyer, especially the Roger Ebert–penned *Beyond the Valley of the Dolls* (1970).

Myra initiates her lesbian relationship with Mary-Ann only after she has raped Rusty with a dildo. This rape inaugurates his transformation from Mary-Ann's resolutely heterosexual partner and stud wannabe, to violent gigolo as kept boy of Letitia Van Allen, Hollywood's premier talent agent, to Ace Mann, television and film star and "complete homosexual" (*Myra Breckinridge*, 212) at the novel's end. Myra's mission to re-create the sexes is inextricable from her desire to restore Hollywood film to its glory days of 1940s studio-dominated production.

As Myra sees it, her sexual mission has been made more urgent by the demise of classic film. From her base of operations at the academy, she surveys her students, whose language, dress code, and behavior are inspired by television, and compares them to the youth of the 1940s: "In the Forties, American Boys created a world empire because they chose to be James Stewart, Clark Gable and William Eythe. By imitating godlike autonomous men, our boys were able to defeat Hitler, Mussolini and Tojo. Could we do it again?" (*Myra Breckinridge*, 34). In this passage, and in many like it, Myra takes for granted that people imitate the role models that they absorb in their encounters with small and big screens. The success of Myra's mission, to restore the power of the studios and revolutionize the sexes, depends, however, on a differently mediated imitation: her literary self-creation. Insistent on writing her own remarkable and disturbing beauty first, Myra hopes to accomplish the creation of a literary masterpiece as the first necessary step toward re-creating the sexes.

Myra's self-creation as a "literary masterpiece" is fulfilled by her conjuring herself into visibility through the evocation of film images (her breasts "reminiscent of those sported by Jean Harlow"). Myra's missions may rely on the circuit that Vidal establishes between the page and the big screen, but they are ultimately achieved, as the sequel, *Myron*, makes clear, because of the status of the television. *Myra Breckinridge* ends with Myra, now Myron once again, having been hit by a car and surgically restored to masculinity, married to Mary-Ann, living a "happy and normal life" in the San Fernando Valley, "raising dogs and working for Planned Parenthood" (213). We might expect a sequel for no other reason than because evidence of Myra's existence is perpetuated, despite these appearances, in Myron's profession: he writes a television series for ABC. Both novels are fully informed by the position that TV holds in the circuit Vidal establishes between print and film.

Myron, which begins where *Myra* leaves off, clarifies the relations between film and television even as it represents more complex relations between pre- and postoperative sexual identities. *Myron* negotiates a complicated temporal scheme between the time of Myron's headlong entry into the television set in 1973 during a late-night screening of *Siren of Babylon*, a fictional Maria Montez vehicle, and 1948, the time of the filming of *Siren of Babylon*. Set almost entirely inside the television, the novel is structured by the struggle between Myra and Myron as each vies for control of the same body. Each chapter is alternately narrated by Myron, who has moved from the valley to a comfortable Brentwood home, to which he longs to return to resume his "normal" life, and Myra, always the megalomaniac, who wants to restore, not only her own "once and future" beautiful breasts, but, along with them, the heyday of classic Hollywood cinema.

Even before coming into competition with her remasculinized preoperative identity in *Myron*, Myra had in *Myra Breckinridge* differentiated herself from Myron along intellectual as well as sexual lines. Although she shared with Myron an admiration for the work of the film critic Parker Tyler:

> I am not Myron Breckinridge but myself and despite the intensely symbiotic relationship my husband and I enjoyed during his brief life and despite the fact that I entirely support his thesis that the films of 1935 to 1945 inclusive were the high point of Western culture, completing what began that day in the theater of Dionysos when Aeschylus first spoke to the Athenians, I must confess that I part company with Myron on the subject of TV. In fact, I was sufficiently *avant-garde* in 1959 to recognize the fact that it was no longer the movies but the television commercial that engaged the passionate attention of the world's best artists and technicians.

Moreover: "The relationship between consumer and advertiser is the last demonstration of *necessary* love in the West, and its principal form of expression is the television commercial" (30).

The relations of competition between film and TV, here voiced by Myra, are made more prominent in the "through-the-looking-glass" world of *Myron*, in which all the characters who have entered the television at various points at which the movie has been televised are perpetually stuck in a time loop: the duration of the filming of *Siren of Babylon*. Capitalizing on being trapped in 1948, Myra hopes to make contact with the heads of MGM Studios and use the benefits of hindsight to prevent the eclipse of the studio system. But she must also outwit Mr. Williams, the man in the back office, the earliest TV viewer to be transported back to 1948 from 1950. Using his insider knowledge from the future, Mr. Williams helps guarantee the declining box office of MGM's post-1948 film production at the same time as he manages the lives of those TV viewers trapped in 1948. He seeks to use TV to ruin film in order to restore the primacy of print. Myra, by contrast, aims to use TV to recapitalize MGM and prevent the stepping down of Louis B. Mayer in 1952.

One of the constraints on the characters who have entered their televisions is that they are forbidden to interrupt the filming of the movie; indeed, they are invisible to the participants in the making of the film while they are on the film set. Needless to say, these constraints are overcome by Myra, who discovers that, during commercial breaks, the world of the film set is frozen and the film's participants can be touched and their positions even subtly altered while they remain totally unaware of outside interference. Myra takes advantage of this possibility for contact by baring the Babylonian extras' breasts and asses for brief moments. She thus manages through subliminal seduction of the TV viewer to retroactively increase the studio's revenues. Vidal's representation of the competition between film and TV and between both screens and print puts all three venues onto a circuit, suggesting that it is no longer possible to opt exclusively for one or the other.

Ultimately, Myra slips a card into the foreskin of a red-headed extra named Steve Dude, thereby setting up a date. Myra plans, after having sodomized Steve, to transform him by sex surgery into a "sterile fun-loving Amazon [who will be] the ideal identity for every red-blooded American boy" (*Myron*, 324). Meeting with Steve and Sydney Spaceman, a casting man at MGM, Myra tries to sell the idea of a film in which "Steve is turned into a girl before our very eyes":

> We'll even show the operation. After all, you can't cheat the audience. Naturally the surgery will be in Good Taste and should occur no later than the second reel. From then on we tell a happy story, the life not of Steve but of Stephanie—a joyous fun-loving sterile Amazon, living a perfect life *without* children, and so an example to the youth of the world, a model for every young male, and our salvation, humanity's as well as Metro's. (373)

Sydney responds: "I don't get you honey. I mean maybe there's some box office in something so gruesome, like Frankenstein. But what's the lesson for the youth of the world?" In response, Myra begins a rant about overpopulation whose Malthusian logic underwrites the peculiar version of the sexual revolution into which she had inducted Rusty and Mary-Ann in *Myra Breckinridge*, but she stops, wisely realizing that the thought of the approaching end of the human race is "too new in the pre-Myra 1948" (373). Myra attempts to sell Sydney Spaceman her movie, comparing it favorably to a sequel to *Mrs. Miniver* (1942) then in the making. But Myra's pitch seems more suitable for a TV series than a film. Indeed, series TV would be the ideal form for imparting the lessons of her peculiar brand of sexual liberation.

Myron ultimately finds the way out of the television set by following two men who are dragging between them a third, who is wearing a Richard Nixon mask, forcing him out the exit; the third man *is* Richard Nixon. Nixon, seeking refuge from the Watergate scandal, wants to know: "Is there an extradition treaty between 1948 and the future?" (*Myron*, 310). Despite his effort to use TV to his own advantage, Nixon is rapidly ushered back into 1973. Tuned into the way in which TV worked against Nixon, Vidal relies on his readers' awareness that the Watergate scandal represented a high-water mark for the role of television in American politics.

Myron, an ardent Nixon supporter, is too distracted by the opportunity to escape and so does not notice Nixon's admission of guilt. Myron has to bide his time to escape while Myra controls their body—she even temporarily *becomes* Maria Montez—but, when he does reensconce himself in Brentwood, we are treated to a wonderful set of revisions. On his return, he finds that John F. Kennedy, the senator from Massachusetts and brother-in-law of Marilyn Monroe, is about to begin a presidential race against Stephanie Dude, a fun-loving Amazon and the Republican nominee. Myra has changed history by operating through the television set.

The alternative political history that Vidal has Myra make possible is an elaborate joke, but one that turns on the perception that sexuality is central to politics. Retroactively circumventing the Watergate scandal, Nixon and his entire administration have been eliminated from U.S. political history, and Nixon has been replaced by the transsexual Republican Party nominee Stephanie Dude. Both Kennedy assassinations seem also to have been averted, and the Camelot moment has been both deferred to 1973 and deidealized, its ethos having been made more sexually explicit with the marriage of RFK to Marilyn Monroe. Not only is this alternative political history made possible because of the setting of the action of *Myron* inside the television set, but Myra's revisionary interference is also enabled by the commercial breaks in the television screening of the late-late movie. Vidal thus makes good on Myra's claim that television commercials are the last demonstration of necessary love in the West.

The Erotic Current of TV

In his initial considerations of television, Vidal had claimed that the book was still necessary: according to the introduction to the 1956 publication of a collection of his television dramas, the book provides the only repository for a body of work otherwise consigned to ephemeral status, whose record in the pre–video age existed only on kinescope.[1] Although much in *Screening History*, *Myra Breckinridge*, and *Myron* would seem to suggest that film replaces the book as historical record, television, rather than film, becomes the archive for

Vidal. Allied with memory, film shares the problem of forgetfulness that gives rise to Vidal's mock elegiac tone in *Screening History* and in his renaming of his country the United States of Amnesia. But, if in *Myra Breckinridge* and *Myron* TV usurps the book's role as historical record, in *Live from Golgotha* it comes to constitute the archive itself.

Curiously, the germ of *Golgotha* is contained in a passage in the earlier *Myron*. When Myra encounters the movie stars William Eythe and Lon ("Bud") McCallister on the road that runs around the perimeter of the film set, she describes their car and becomes strangely self-conscious:

> In it were two young men. Note how calmly, how simply, I record this information. It is as if St. Paul were starting to tell *his* tall tale with the casual remark that "while making good time one morning on the road to Damascus, I happened to see this funny-looking specimen standing on the side of the road—a hitchhiker, I thought." (321)

Golgotha is narrated from the perspective, not of Paul, but of Timothy, bishop of Macedonia, even though Paul/Saul often has occasion in the novel to comment on his experiences on the Damascus freeway and the appearance of a fat Jesus. A hilarious satire on the millenarianisms of our day and those of the decades following the death of Christ, *Golgotha*, like *Myron*, features the television set as the vehicle for time travel. Indeed, Vidal invites us to understand *Live from Golgotha* as an extended meditation on the New Age concept of "channeling"—Shirley MacLaine even makes an appearance in A.D. 96

to receive her due recognition as the popularizer of this concept.[2]

Exponentially complicating the temporal scheme of *Myron*, *Golgotha*'s premise is that a hacker has erased all tapes of the New Testament except for one, which will become the sole version, the "Gospel according to Gore Vidal," as the novel is subtitled, because the hacker's sabotage has also erased from memory, and thus from history, all the events surrounding the establishment of early Christianity. As Timothy composes his memoirs, he receives unexpected visits from various twentieth-century luminaries—some real, such as Mary Baker Eddy, the founder of Christian Science, and some fictive, such as the NBC television executives and technicians— all of whom seek both to guarantee the continued existence of Christian doctrine and to produce a version that confirms their own individual beliefs.

Golgotha puts a postmodern spin on the Christian tenet that the Bible is the Word of God. Timothy and the other apostles speak fluent entertainment-industry hucksterese even before the installation of television in their milieu, but the influence from the future of television viewing and "channeling" turns the crucifixion into cruci-fiction as the history of the dissemination of early Christianity becomes hopelessly entangled with input from the present. Even though computer technology is the source of the scrambling and erasure of "truth," it is television and video technologies, and the time travel that they permit, that make it possible for the events to occur as well as providing the only possible grounds for their interpretation. Ultimately, then, the televisual apparatus becomes the vehicle for redemption, but Vidal's satire empties redemption and millenarianism of any theological significance and posits in its place a this-worldly redemption of memory, history, and Japanese-owned entertainment. In *Myra Breckinridge* and *Myron*, as we have seen, Vidal recuperates and reorients the sexual meanings that the term *boob tube* engenders and, against all expectations, establishes television as *the* archive of history and memory. He takes up the implications of television's supersession of the book (and the Book) in *Golgotha*.

Although the narrative trajectory in which TV replaces the book paves the way for ruminations on cultural loss, Vidal's satires undermine our confidence that things were any better before TV. Indeed, for Vidal, books and TV seem to be on a continuum. No simple love or hatred of print or electronic media can be extracted from his treatments. But according to Marshall McLuhan, the original media theorist, people have failed to appreciate TV because they insist on understanding TV in terms of books.

For McLuhan, TV is a highly participatory medium that demands a creative response from its viewers. Critiquing the conventional view that TV presents an experience for passive viewers, McLuhan analyzed the role of television in the aftermath of the Kennedy assassination: "The guards who failed to protect Lee Oswald were not passive. They were so involved by the mere sight of the TV cameras that they lost their sense of their merely practical and specialist task." For McLuhan, it's TV's low information density, the feature that elicits creative viewer participation, that makes it a "cool" medium:

> Perhaps it was the Kennedy funeral that most strongly impressed the audience with the power of TV to invest an occasion with the character of corporate participation. Most of all, the Kennedy event provides an opportunity for noting a paradoxical feature of the "cool" TV medium. It involves us in moving depth, but it does not excite, agitate or arouse. Presumeably this is a feature of all depth experience.[3]

McLuhan contrasts cool, low-information-density media like TV with hot, high-information-density media like print and film. McLuhan rightly objects to treatments of TV that use print-based criteria, but his strange use of *depth* to describe that which elicits affectless involvement and his reliance on oppositions such as *hot* and *cool* signify that he conceptualizes only the differences between print and electronic media. Vidal is more interested in their similarities. He renders the contrast between hot and cool media in a moment in *Myron* that explodes McLuhan's opposition of books and TV. The *Myron* moment clarifies the circuit of relations between the page, the television, and the film screen even as it exposes an erotic current running along that circuit.

Before Myra can get to work on her plan to sexually transform Steve, she first has to negotiate the limits on her potential for interference with the 1948 world, limits that stem from her own attitudes toward film and its star system. Catching sight, as we have seen, of two young men whom she recognizes as William Eythe and Lon McCallister, she runs, screaming, after their car. Maude, her male hairdresser companion, soothes her after they peel off: "Sweetie, you've got to get used to movie stars. They drive along here all the time" (*Myron*, 321). Myra is, in her own words, "for once, silenced by emotion":

> How could I ever express to this Paganini of hair—to anyone—what it is that I feel about those two mythic youths now seen by me in the actual flesh at the height of their glory and *in the round*—an effect so far not truly possible in the movies despite various attempts like *House of Wax*, where one was obliged to hold up cardboard spectacles containing red and green celluloid in order to get a sense of the third dimension whose absence—and one must face this fact squarely—has *made* the art of cinema unique and glorious, for in its very flatness celluloid is as complete and final as the walls of the Sistine Chapel or of the Radio City Music Hall. Yes, as two-dimensional and triumphantly flat as a page of the *Divine Comedy*. To give either the movies or the pages of a classic actual depth would be to mar perfection, to make confusion where all is now clarity. Yet, I confess, that for me to see *in person* movie stars of yesteryear *in yesteryear* is something else again, and creates euphoria. (322)

Myra's emotional outburst reveals that film, like literature and painting, McLuhan's hot media, attains classic status through the clarity of flatness. Television, by contrast, a round medium—a tube—provides different, euphoria-inducing access to history, a type of access in which classic status is, perhaps, irrelevant. Like Myra, Vidal is willing to exploit the tube's access to history—in print. Vidal's dramatic rendering of McLuhan's contrast between hot and cool media prefers flatness and roundness to depth. Myra's excited ravings also capture the sexy edge of cool that seems to have eluded McLuhan. And Vidal is not the only one who perceives that TV can elicit sexual response.

As early as 1954, the noted French film theorist André Bazin suggested that television had an erotic logic. In "Contributions toward an Erotic Logic of Television," Bazin observed that TV broadcasting, always "live" at that time, had the potential for showing things that the producers may not have intended.[4] For Bazin, the viewer's unforeseen encounter with the accidental was a breakthrough of "real" time into the familial, desexualized space of the living room. These accidents, he suggested, disrupt domestic intimacies with an eroticism all the more intense because they are unforeseen and interruptive. The TV, in his view, thus provides more exciting viewing pleasures than those offered in the cinema. Bazin's prime example of such an accidental erotic encounter is not, as one might expect, an inadvertent glimpse of a breast but, rather, the sight of Queen Elizabeth II's exhaustion during her coronation. It may be hard to recollect that the queen once had sex appeal, but you don't have to be J. G. Ballard to imagine the erotic charge that would have accompanied any TV footage of the car crash that killed Princess Diana.

In *The Philosophy of Andy Warhol*, Warhol goes further, representing the television as a lover. Keeping "the television on all the time, especially while people were telling [him] their problems," solves Warhol's problem of picking up other people's problems that had prompted a visit to a psychiatrist: TV, by "some kind of magic," overrides or diverts the transmission of other people's problems (23–24). The "magic" of impersonal contact, like that of anonymous sex, sustains the affair that he carries on with television, "which has continued to the present, when I play around in my bedroom with as many as four at a time," even though he is married to his tape-recorder, which he calls "my wife" (26).

Drawing together Warhol's thoughts on work, ambition, fame, money, sex, and love, the *Philosophy* devotes three sections to love in which television figures prominently. In the third section, Warhol confesses that he is a very jealous person. His description of the way in which this jealousy surfaces suggests a possible explanation of the apparent affectlessness and incoherence of his public appearance, at least on television: "The few times in my life when I've gone on television, I've been so jealous of the host on the show that I haven't been able to talk. As soon as the TV cameras turn on, all I can think is, 'I want my own show. . . . I want my own show'" (50). This topic recurs frequently, and Warhol reiterates his acknowledgment of "the great unfulfilled ambition of my life: my own regular TV show. I'm going to call it *Nothing Special*" (6): "As I said, I want a show of my own—called *Nothing Special*" (147). This witty title exploits the idiomatic response to the question, "What's on?" by drawing attention to the special nothingness that television routinely offers and promising to elevate it, if only typographically by capitalizing the first letter of each word, to a new plateau. Indeed, the phrase *nothing special* comprises Warhol's philosophy of love in which making nothing happen ensures both sexual satisfaction and fame (50). For Warhol: "Sex is more exciting on the screen and between the pages than between the sheets" (44). In contrast with the telephone, "the most intimate and exclusive of all media," which Warhol prefers above face-to-face communication as a form of "contact with your closest friends," television offers the ideal combination of sexual excitement and fame because it is the "least exclusive" (146) of media.

Bazin, Warhol, and Vidal, like Jacqueline Susann in *The Love Machine*, all managed to appreciate and exploit the shift from print to screen modes of publicity even as they recognized and responded to TV as an erotic transmitter. Indeed, these commentators traverse print and screen media by erotic pathways; once we let them guide us, it's possible to observe in many other places the association of TV with sexual arousal even if it gets expressed only in the negative register, as TV's sexual threat.

Lifting a page from nineteenth-century antimasturbation tracts, parents continue to warn their children not to sit too close to the TV or they will ruin their eyes. No scientific study has ever been conducted to investigate this potential hazard. The injunction registers TV's sexual threat, as do a range of slang terms for the television: the *box*, the *tube*, the *boob tube*. "It's hard to imagine going to bed with anything other than

The Tonight Show": such statements crop up regularly in discussions of late-night television, although the sexual aspects of TV are not usually remarked.[5] Indeed, recurrent scenes on that excellent satire of late-night talk shows, *The Larry Sanders Show*, featured the eponymous television host, Larry Sanders (Gary Shandling), too distracted by his own appearance on TV to complete the seduction of the woman in bed beside him. It is hard to tell if Larry's narcissistic impairment would be rendered more or less abject if he actually were to have sex in those scenes, but their satiric efficacy depends, nevertheless, on the location of the TV in the master bedroom. This migration of the TV from the family room to the master bedroom has remained, for the most part, unnoticed, though it suggests that the eroticism of the TV observed by Bazin in 1954 has become, like so much else in our culture, more sexually explicit.

When Vidal and his contemporaries treat TV as another erogenous zone, they imagine an erotic arousal that is unnatural. When popular idiom and parental warnings ward off TV's sexual threat, they would inoculate TV viewers from the unnatural, passive eroticism that TV supposedly induces. Both celebrations and castigations recognize TV as a sexual supplement, but some treatments refuse to ascribe the effects of the medium to its technology. The multiple transformations of Myron-Myra—from masculinity to femininity, male to female, and back again—problematize the senses in which genes or genitals determine sexual identity or behavior, suggesting instead that power is the key factor. Likewise, in Vidal's treatments, TV's technological features are irrelevant to its uses; who owns it is of overriding political significance. Vidal's writings thus display a congruence between the refusal of genetic (or genital) determinism in the domain of sexuality and technological determinism in the domain of publicity. The eroticism of TV in Vidal and his contemporaries' writings points to another lesson: that it is in the attribution of inherent meaning to the medium itself (be it TV or sexuality) that we prematurely limit its multiple potential uses and thus limit as well our opportunities to have sex and appear on TV.

Televisual Classicism

It would be a mistake, however, to see Vidal's use of TV only in terms of the 1960s, sexual liberation, and the rise of identity politics. Vidal does not view TV as either observer or participant, the dichotomy that structures the responses of the panelists assessing the legacy of 1968 for TV. Nor does he accept the sexual identity that Buckley would confer on him.

In his *Esquire* piece, Buckley gave a survey of his conflicts with Vidal and saw fit to quote a telegram that he composed but never sent to Jack Paar following a fight that he and Vidal had had on *The Tonight Show* in 1962 over the relations between the pope and American law:

PLEASE INFORM GORE VIDAL THAT NEITHER I NOR MY FAMILY IS DISPOSED TO RECEIVE LESSONS IN MORALITY FROM A PINK QUEER. IF HE WISHES TO CHALLENGE THAT DESIGNATION, INFORM HIM THAT I SHALL FIGHT BY THE

LAWS OF THE MARQUIS OF QUEENSBURY. ("On Experiencing Gore Vidal," 109)

If Buckley could be said to have forced Vidal to deal with the
ways in which politics and sexuality could be connected in
1968, issuing him the invitation to become the Oscar Wilde
of his day, it can now be made clear why Vidal declined.

A case could be made that Wilde's mastery of specifically
print-based forms of publicity should be seen as part and
parcel of his having come to be the emblem for homosexual
identity, the patron saint of identity-based sexual politics in
the 1960s.[6] Indeed, Christopher Hitchens champions Wilde's
treatments of socialism as more suitable now, in a world after
the fall of the Berlin Wall, than they may have been in their
own time (*Unacknowledged Legislation*, 15). But, for Vidal,
Wilde represents a moment that is only of confined historical
interest rather than any immediate political relevance. Hitchens compares Wilde to Vidal (8), a comparison that Vidal
might find irritating, for Vidal goes back over Wilde's head,
framing him as of specific historical interest by drawing attention to the conjuncture, in Wilde, of a homosexual identity
and specific media conditions.

In "Oscar Wilde: On the Skids Again" (1987), Vidal as-
serts that the revolution in consciousness usually associated
with the 1960s really began in the 1940s with "the war and
Kinsey, penicillin and The Pill" (*Sexually Speaking*, 149).
Even though Vidal here made a rare error (he is wrong about
the Pill, which was given FDA approval only in 1960), the pro-
vocative gesture to backdate the sexual revolution, prompted

by his universalizing understanding of sexuality, is worth considering, for it aims to circumvent the identity politics associated with the legacy of the 1960s in the domains of both sexuality and the media. Vidal frequently uses the 1940s as a lens through which to view the 1960s. *Myra Breckinridge* and its sequel repeatedly juxtapose the ethos, imagery, and language of the 1960s to those of the 1940s, whose films, according to Myra, inspired "our boys . . . to defeat Hitler, Mussolini and Tojo." Although Vidal's investments in the 1940s have struck some as stemming only from nostalgia for the period of his youth, his thinking through the 1960s in terms of the 1940s affords the opportunity to return to Foucault's layering of post-1945 onto post-1968 in giving the history of the intellectual.[7]

Vidal's joint embrace of nonidentitarian sexual politics and the most contemporary media brackets and suspends Wilde, both as a homosexual identity and as a print-based intellectual, as an example from a modern epoch that is past. As an exemplary intellectual, Wilde was affiliated with print and the live performances of the lecture circuit, the theater, and the law courts, but not with screened performance. Vidal's practice of the intellectual career suggests that the discovery in 1968 of TV as a participant in rather than observer of events, and the flourishing of identity politics since then, also belongs to the past modern moment exemplified by Wilde. This mode of understanding the intellectual inadvertently privileges print media, live-ness, and a collapse of the distinctions between culture and politics as politics are mobilized around fixed identities, whether of race, sexuality, gender, or even media. The period that this understanding of the intellectual enshrines spans much of the twentieth century, during which electronic forms of publicity had concurrently become available. But who says ways of thinking about culture, or its modes of classification, keep pace with scientific and social changes? As the case of Vidal suggests, this way of understanding the intellectual, hobbled as it is by an investment in fixing either the identity or the medium itself, will properly account neither for the advent of the writer-intellectual to screen cultures nor, more crucially, for the overlaps between print and screen modes of publicity.

132

As Vidal's own treatment of Wilde indicates, his preferred frame of reference for the nexus of sexuality and politics is, not the moment of sexual liberation just pre- and post-Stonewall (a long moment that could include the queer activism of the last decade), but the world of Rome. James Tatum has given a persuasive exposition of Vidal's adherence to the world of Rome, which he calls Vidal's *Romanitas*.[8] Underwriting Vidal's *Romanitas* is a universalism evident in his treatments of sexuality but also there in his mode of political address. The example of Vidal should thus prompt an alternative account of the intellectual and the media that would consider the prospects of universalism in our day.

Perversely, perhaps, when I call Vidal's intellectual career an *exercise in televisual classicism* I take my cue from the man whom Vidal obliterated from his alternative political history of the United States: Richard Nixon. It was Nixon who recognized and confirmed Vidal's classic status. When asked to what purposes he would put the auditorium of his presidential library, Nixon said that it should be used to reenact "great debates like—oh, Vidal and Buckley" (Hitchens, *Unacknowledged Legislation*, 70–71). Vidal and Buckley's 1968 battle had brought sexuality into the political arena, something the noncharismatic, conservative Nixon would seem the least likely to have recognized, but here Nixon confers on Vidal and Buckley the status of national treasures.

Vidal's classicism consists of a universalizing understanding of both sexuality and publicity accompanied by a strong sense of history that registers changes in the status that has been accorded to each. Others account for such changes by attributing them to features of the thing undergoing the change: in the case of sex, the discovery of sexual identity, for example; or, in the case of the media of publicity, either print's purported independence from the market or TV's market orientation. Arguing against these determinisms, Vidal understands that these changes arise, not from any inherent feature of the thing itself, but from the ways in which they are used under different particular configurations of state power and society.

Against all expectations framed by the contemporary understanding of TV, Vidal is able to yoke classicism to TV, the vehicle through which his politics (and sexual politics) frequently have been expressed. This combination, on display throughout his career, is also visible in the recent pamphleteering, in which he revives the form of writing most closely associated with active and virtuous citizenship in a republic, on the one hand, and avails himself of the newest configuration of electronic sources and audiences, on the other. Vidal dedicates *Dreaming War* (2002) to "Publius, the joint authors of *The Federalist*, in whose words our republic truly began."[9] In his bestselling *9-11*, Noam Chomsky responded to a question about how the role of social activists may have been altered by the 9/11 terrorist attacks by commenting that, since then, he has had considerably more access, even to mainstream U.S. media, than ever before.[10] Vidal self-consciously allies himself with Chomsky in "Menandering towards Armageddon," his response to the *New Yorker* writer Louis Menand's accusations that he is a conspiracy theorist.[11] Both men are the beneficiaries of a new media opportunity: even as official print and broadcast sources in the United States have become more homogeneous and propagandistic, many more people than would identify themselves as radicals are availing themselves of international print and broadcast resources on the Web.[12] This configuration, as Chomsky's comments register, provides both him and Vidal access to a new broad-based audience, which, to this point, they have chosen to consolidate through print publication in pamphlet form.

In Vidal's resuscitation of a literary form associated with classical republicanism for current political use, we see a textual counterpart to his surprising discovery that TV can supplement the universal intellectual. Both moves suggest that there may be untapped potentials for democratic politics in a post-Enlightenment universalism that are not at odds with history but work within it. This discovery has allowed Vidal to maintain the position of an intellectual for the past forty years and should be factored back into current accounts of the intellectual. If Vidal has declined to be the Wilde of his day, it's because he has been Myra instead.

Myra Redux?

If, led by Myra's memorable outrageousness, Vidal has imagined a radical utopia in fiction, he has also appeared in public *as* Myra partly as a result of his understanding of TV. Although Vidal has had his Myron moments in which he disdains television, as he did in the 1985 *New Left Review* interview when he claimed, "I never watch television, but I know all about it" ("Surrealism and Patriotism," 99), he has also had his Myra moments: for example, in the 1974 *Gay Sunshine* interview when he reoriented Myra's claim that television commercials are the last demonstration of necessary love in the West in his own voice. When asked about the prospect of changing society through film rather than through the printed word, Vidal stated: "No. I don't think that any film nowadays can have the slightest influence in the ways those films had when everybody went to the movies. The equivalent today would be TV commercials." The exchange continued:

> GS: An Industry where some of our most creative people master the art of subliminal seduction.
> GV: Yeah. A television series, maybe. I'm sure that *All in the Family* and *Mary Tyler Moore* have had more impact on American mores. But you won't see the impact for ten to twenty years, the same way as you did not see

the influence of Hollywood in my generation. (*Sexually Speaking*, 248)

The differences in tone between Myra and Vidal should not distract us from their shared observation that screen media affect mores. Moreover, Vidal, like Myra, locates TV—both series programming and commercials—as the site most likely to usher in political change.

If Myra provides Vidal with the linchpin between romance and history, between the screen and the page, she also offers a special perspective on some idiosyncratic features of Vidal's writing. I have earmarked throughout the preceding pages certain recurrences: the reappearance of plot elements in *Washington, D.C.* originally developed in the last Edgar Box mystery; the premise of *Myron* in "Top Ten Best-Sellers of January, 1973"; the premise of *Golgotha* in the pages of *Myron*; the premise of *Screening History* in "Top Ten Best-Sellers." I would suggest that these recurrences of phrases, plot turns, characters, and chunks of reasoning in various formats are the remnants of Vidal's serious literary ambition.

Literary allusion, the hallmark of literary seriousness, relies for its effects on readers' memory and permits writers to situate themselves in relation to the literary tradition through the selective appropriation and revision of other writers' words. The obverse of literary allusion, Vidal's self-citation capitalizes on readerly amnesia even as it insists on a certain kind of fame. Vidal both presumes a loyal readership that enjoys him in all venues and counts on his readers' forgetting. This gesture would thus seem to appropriate for the page the star-vehicle status of the silver screen. If readers miss a few of his performances, which, like those of Joan Crawford or Bette Davis, are all indexed to one another, or tune in late, to switch the metaphor to TV, he guarantees that they will not be missing much.

Indeed, Vidal's habit of self-citation exhibits his ambivalence toward amnesia: he exploits public amnesia even as he guards against its effects. At these moments, the page seems to operate like the film screen in *Screening History*, mediating characters' voices and authorial political or literary commentary, which, like personal memory and social history, become similarly indistinguishable. An outstanding example of this self-citation occurs in the 1971 "Women's Liberation: Feminism and Its Discontents."

That essay gives a sympathetic account of second-wave feminist classics such as Kate Millett's *Sexual Politics* (1970) and Eva Figes's *Patriarchal Attitudes* (1970). Vidal proposes that feminism's critique of the patriarchal family, "this new desire to exist not as male or female but as human," is actually a response, albeit an unself-conscious one, to overpopulation:

> We are breeding ourselves into extinction. We cannot feed the people now alive. In thirty-seven years the world's population will double unless we have the "good luck" to experience on the grandest scale famine, plague, war. To survive we must stop making babies at the current rate, and this can only be accomplished by breaking the stereotypes of man the warrior, woman the breeder. (*United States*, 593)

This updated version of Malthus, with its odd precision—"in thirty-seven years"—sounds, perhaps, less ridiculous in the mouth of Myra Breckinridge, who uses the same logic to seduce Rusty and Mary-Ann into broadening their sexual horizons. Here's Myra:

> Then I gave statistics for the current world death rate, showing how it has drastically declined in the last fifty years due to advanced medicine. As a result of miracle drugs and incontinent breeding, the world's food supply can no longer support the billions of people alive at present. What is to be done? How is the race to be saved? My answer was simple enough: famine and war are now man's only hope. To survive, the human population must be drastically reduced. "But what can we do to *stop* this from happening?" Mary-Ann was plainly alarmed. "Don't have children. That is the best thing. . . . And try to change your attitude toward what is normal. . . . [T]he only alternative [to nuclear holocaust] would be for all the Rustys to follow the Spartan custom of making love to boys, while the Mary-Anns, as lovers of women, would at least help to preserve the race by bringing no more children into the world. (*Myra Breckinridge*, 120–23)

Myra's inimitable voice is hardly inimitable when Vidal reproduces its argument elsewhere.

The subtitle of "Women's Liberation"—"Feminism and Its Discontents"—alludes to Freud's *Civilization and Its Discontents* (1930). This is not Vidal's only allusion to Freud, despite the resolute anti-Freudianism that he also espouses. A deep reliance on Freudian terms, including screen memory and the unconscious, evident in the oedipal scenario in the 1995 preface to *The City and the Pillar* and in the description of American political history as family romance in *Screening History*, attests to the iconic status that Freud came to have as a sign of cultural and intellectual authority in the age of sexual revolution. Indeed, such uses of Freud—those that invoke his prestige but divest him of his ideas—are hardly unique to Vidal.

Vidal's allusion to Freud also amplifies his ambivalence about amnesia. The ambivalence about amnesia (and Freud) encoded in self-citation is resolved by adopting a mode of address modeled on the television, the perfect vehicle, as Myra knows, for love (and knowledge) in an amnesiac age. Vidal's self-citations, I would suggest, are structured like TV reruns. They thus provide another instance of the importance of television to Vidal's oeuvre. But, again, such self-citation is hardly unique to Vidal. One might find numerous examples across literary and journalistic writing of the past forty years. Recycling, as Andy Warhol comments in his *Philosophy*, is central to the process of making business art and art business (93).

As exemplary analyst of the media shift from print to screen, Vidal sutures print and screen modes of publicity. His analysis of the media shift, like his practice of working across media, outlines the contours of the intellectual career in the age of TV. Vidal uses TV in two ways: to translate across the divide that appears to separate print from screen cultures and to provide the mode of address for practicing politics, including sexual politics, in a nonidentitarian register. This doubleness has made it particularly rewarding to bring a consideration of Vidal's career to the question of the intellectual, especially when the distinctions between politics and culture that have collapsed in identity politics inform much current academic work, both on TV and on sexuality. Vidal's uses of TV run counter to the narratives of its having ruined intellectual and political debate.

The tantalizing possibility that Myra really speaks for Vidal or Vidal for Myra, like many questions of literary voice, remains ultimately undecidable. Vidal's signal contribution is to brilliantly illuminate the conditions that make it so: the current cultural matrix that determines that we can't distinguish among history, memory, what we have seen on either big or small screens or on the page. Bemoaning the demise of the serious novel, or the disintegration of literary fame, as the consequence of the loss of history makes Vidal's satirical stance reminiscent of Alexander Pope's. He thus might seem to support those who believe in the decline of the intellectual or of literary seriousness. But Vidal simultaneously overrides Pope's famous definition of wit — "What oft was thought but ne'er so well expressed" — by expressing it so well, so often, verbatim. Such reproduction, enabled by the central position of television in Vidal's writing, points to the future possibilities suggested by Myra's utopian mission, to "re-create the sexes and thus save the human race from certain extinction." Exploiting the television commercial as "the last demonstration of *necessary* love in the West," Vidal successfully negotiates a public role for the author as intellectual on the basis of the circuit that he establishes between the page and the movie screen, a circuit that relies on the mediation of that amnesia-inducing and immortality-producing medium: the television. Vidal uses TV to ward off the blurring of the boundaries between culture and politics in identity-based politics. He exploits the congruencies among critiques of genetic, genital, and technological determinism. By these means, he has refused to be ghettoized — less, however, as a gay man than as a specific intellectual. In TV he has found both a vehicle through which to convey his politics and a mode of address for a new televisual public, that is, a public conditioned by television even when it reads. Vidal's career teaches us that it is possible to remain a universal intellectual in the age of TV. He has done so by negotiating the print-screen circuit.

Notes

After the first full citation in the notes, page numbers for subsequent citations have been given in the text.

Introduction

1   Gore Vidal, *Screening History* (Cambridge: Harvard University Press, 1992), 2–3.
2   Arthur Meier Schlesinger Jr., *A Life in the Twentieth Century*, 1 vol. to date (Boston: Houghton Mifflin, 2000–), 140.

1   The Print Intellectual

1   Gore Vidal, *United States: Essays, 1952–1992* (New York: Random House, 1993), 1156–57.
2   Bruce Robbins, *Feeling Global: Internationalism in Distress* (New York: New York University Press, 1999), chap. 1; and Carl Rollyson and Lisa Paddock, *Susan Sontag: The Making of an Icon* (New York: Norton, 2000).
3   Edward Said, *Representations of the Intellectual: The 1993 Reith Lectures* (New York: Random House, 1994), 70.

4   Richard A. Posner, *Public Intellectuals: A Study of Decline* (Cambridge: Harvard University Press, 2001).

5   "How and Where to Find [the] Intellectual Elite in the United States," *Public Opinion Quarterly* 35 (1971): 18 n. 1.

6   Neil Postman, *Amusing Ourselves to Death: Public Discourse in the Age of Show Business* (New York: Viking, 1985).

7   Pierre Bourdieu, *On Television* (1996), trans. Priscilla Parkhurst Ferguson (New York: New Press, 1998).

8   Michael Walzer takes up the distinction, even though he offers a critique of Foucault's theory of power, in *The Company of Critics: Social Criticism and Political Commitment in the Twentieth Century* (New York: Basic, 1988).

9   Michel Foucault, *Power/Knowledge: Selected Interviews and Other Writings, 1972–1977*, ed. Colin Gordon, trans. Colin Gordon et al. (New York: Pantheon, 1980), 127. It is worth noting that the material quoted in the text is Foucault's written answer to an interviewer's question and that the emphasis is his.

10 For one such account that locates the beginning of the 1960s in 1958 and usefully identifies the tactics and terms that such identity-based political movements took from Third World decolonization, see Fredric Jameson, "Periodizing the 60s," *Social Text* 9–10 (spring-summer 1984): 178–209.

11 David Foster Wallace, "E Unibus Pluram: Television and U.S. Fiction" (1993), in *A Supposedly Fun Thing I'll Never Do Again: Essays and Arguments* (Boston: Little, Brown, 1997), 27.

12 Jonathan Franzen, "Perchance to Dream: In the Age of Images, a Reason to Write Novels," *Harper's*, April 1996, 35–54.

13 But Vidal's non sequitur may have been motivated by his recollection of a letter that Henry James wrote about the dinner to Mary Cadwalader Jones: "We went (without Henry [Adams]) last night to a big and really quite pompous function at the White House" (Leon Edel, ed., *Henry James: Letters*, vol. 4, *1895–1916* [Cambridge: Harvard University Press/Belknap, 1984], 337).

14   Fred Kaplan, *Gore Vidal: A Biography* (New York: Doubleday, 1999), 766.

15   Gore Vidal, *Myron* (New York: Random House, 1974), 385–86.

2   The Screen Intellectual

1   Andy Warhol, *The Philosophy of Andy Warhol: From A to B and Back Again* (New York: Harcourt Brace Jovanovich, 1975), 26.

2   Wayne Munson, *All Talk: The Talkshow in Media Culture* (Philadelphia: Temple University Press, 1993), 30.

3   Alan Hirsch, *Talking Heads: Political Talk Shows and Their Star Pundits* (New York: St. Martin's, 1991), 12.

4   See Paolo Carpignano, Robin Andersen, Stanley Aronowitz, and William Difazio, "Chatter in the Age of Electronic Reproduction: Talk Television and the 'Public Mind,'" *Social Text* 25–26 (1990): 33–55.

5   Steven D. Stark, *Glued to the Set: The 60s Television Shows and Events That Made Us Who We Are Today* (New York: Free Press, 1997), 186.

6   Virginia Woolf, "Middlebrow," in *Death of the Moth and Other Essays* (Harmondsworth: Penguin, 1961).

7   Michael Korda, "Wasn't She Great?" *New Yorker*, August 14, 1995, 68.

8   Transcript of "Lincoln Story Conference," Norman Lear and Gore Vidal, February 1980, archived at the State Historical Society of Wisconsin. Thanks to Harry Miller, the archivist, for making the materials available.

9   Shawn Levy, *The King of Comedy: The Life and Art of Jerry Lewis* (New York: St. Martin's, 1996).

10   James L. Neibaur and Ted Okuda, *The Jerry Lewis Films: An Analytical Filmography of the Innovative Comic*, with a foreword by Kathleen Freeman (Jefferson, N.C.: McFarland, 1995), 142.

11   Gore Vidal, *Myra Breckinridge* (Boston: Little, Brown, 1968), 30.

12   Jerry Lewis, *The Total Film-Maker* (New York: Random House, 1971), 5.

13   On the role of this distinction in definitions of the intellectual and in

cultural studies, see Francis Mulhern, *Culture/Metaculture* (London: Routledge, 2000).

14 Michael Paul Rogin, *Ronald Reagan, the Movie and Other Episodes in Political Demonology* (Berkeley and Los Angeles: University of California Press, 1987).

15 Connie Bruck, "The Monopolist: How Lew Wasserman Took Over Hollywood," *New Yorker*, April 21–28, 2003, 136–56.

3 A Fine Romance

1 In an interview, Graves said: "*I, Claudius* and *Claudius, the God* took me eight months. I had to get the job done quickly because I was £400 in debt" (*Conversations with Robert Graves*, ed. Frank L. Kershowshi [Jackson: University Press of Mississippi, 1989], 99).

2 Gore Vidal, *Hollywood: A Novel of America in the 1920s* (New York: Random House, 1990), 346–47.

3 Kenneth Anger, *Hollywood Babylon* (San Francisco: Straight Arrow; New York: Simon and Schuster, 1975), 56.

4 Gore Vidal, *1876* (New York: Random House, 1976), 115.

5 Gore Vidal, *Empire* (New York: Random House, 1987), 409.

6 Eve Sedgwick, Judith Butler, and Jonathan Goldberg have described the currents of sexual desire expressed in Cather by her writing across gendered lines of identification. As these critics have argued, Cather's writings make visible the multiple possible alignments of gender, sexuality, and object choice through an exploration of heterosexual desire that is, at the same time, lesbian desire. See Eve Kosofsky Sedgwick, "Across Genders, Across Sexualities: Willa Cather and Others," *South Atlantic Quarterly* 88 (winter 1989): 53–72; Judith Butler, *Bodies That Matter: On the Discursive Limits of Sex* (New York: Routledge, 1993), 143–66; and Jonathan Goldberg, *Willa Cather and Others* (Durham: Duke University Press, 2001).

7 On Cather and Barker, see Goldberg, *Willa Cather and Others*, chap. 3.

On lesbian historical fiction, see Julie Abraham, *Are Girls Necessary? Lesbian Writing and Modern Histories* (New York: Routledge, 1996).

8   It's worth noting that the pseudonym Everard may also allude to James's Captain Everard in *In the Cage* (1898).

9   Katherine Everard [Gore Vidal], *A Star's Progress* (New York: Dutton, 1950), 9.

10 "The *Gay Sunshine* Interview by Steven Abbott and Tom Willenbecher," reprinted in *Sexually Speaking: Collected Sex Writing by Gore Vidal*, ed. Donald Weise (San Francisco: Cleis, 1999), 243.

11 Barbara Seaman, *Lovely Me: The Life of Jacqueline Susann* (New York: Seven Stories, 1996), 297.

12 Michael Korda, "Wasn't She Great," *New Yorker*, August 14, 1995, 72.

13 Jacqueline Susann, *The Love Machine* (New York: Simon and Schuster, 1969), 378.

14 Korda, "Wasn't She Great," 68.

4   The Print-Screen Circuit

1   Gore Vidal, *The City and the Pillar* (New York: Dutton, 1948), rev. ed. (New York: Dutton, 1965), with a new preface (London: Andre Deutsch, 1995).

2   Christopher Hitchens, *Unacknowledged Legislation: Writers in the Public Sphere* (London: Verso, 2000), 60.

3   In the author's note to *United States*, Vidal notes that he had difficulty getting "The Twelve Caesars" published.

4   Alfred C. Kinsey, Wardell B. Pomeroy, and Clyde E. Martin, *Sexual Behavior in the Human Male* (Philadelphia: Saunders, 1948), 617.

5   For Sedgwick, however, there is no way to adjudicate between these viewpoints. Their contradictions have been further vexed by the question of whether sex acts or sexual being is given definitional priority. Most significantly, for Sedgwick, the potent incoherencies of these contradictions have worked together to make all questions of sexuality

pass as problems of knowledge. See Eve Kosofsky Sedgwick, *Episte-mology of the Closet* (Berkeley and Los Angeles: University of California Press, 1990), 40–41, 86–90.

6 William F. Buckley Jr., "On Experiencing Gore Vidal: Can There Be Any Justification in Calling a Man a Queer before Ten Million People on Television?" *Esquire*, August 1969, 107–32; Gore Vidal, "A Distaste-ful Encounter with William F. Buckley Jr.," *Esquire*, September 1969, 140–46.

7 *National Review*, December 31, 2004, 16; *Esquire's Big Book of Great Writing: More Than 70 Years of Celebrated Journalism*, ed. Adrienne Miller (New York: Hearst, 2003).

8 "Surrealism and Patriotism: The Education of an American Novelist," *New Left Review* 149 (1985): 97.

5   TV: Another Erogenous Zone

1 Gore Vidal, *Best Television Plays* (New York: Ballantine, 1956).

2 Gore Vidal, *Live from Golgotha* (New York: Random House, 1992), 86.

3 Marshall McLuhan, *Understanding Media: The Extensions of Man* (1964; Cambridge: MIT Press, 1994), 336–37.

4 André Bazin, "Pour contribuer à une érotologie de la télévision," *Cahiers du cinéma* 7 (1954): 23–30.

5 Stark, *Glued to the Set*, 182.

6 On Wilde's mastery of print-based forms of publicity, see John Stokes, *In the Nineties* (Chicago: University of Chicago Press, 1989); and Jennifer Wicke, *Advertising Fictions: Literature, Advertisement, and So-cial Reading* (New York: Columbia University Press, 1988).

7 Wendy Brown, *Politics Out of History* (Princeton: Princeton Univer-sity Press, 2001), 7. I disagree with Brown's reading of Vidal as a nos-talgist. For Brown, the problem with contemporary politics is that its central questions have depended on modes of historical thinking that should be jettisoned, and she justifies ridding politics of history in the name of Foucault. Vidal's historicist mode of political practice should

be understood instead to provide a viable alternative politics that retains historical understanding.

8   James Tatum, "The *Romanitas* of Gore Vidal," in *Gore Vidal: Writer against the Grain*, ed. Jay Parini (New York: Columbia University Press, 1992), 230.

9   Gore Vidal, *Dreaming War: Blood for Oil and the Cheney-Bush Junta* (New York: Thunder's Mouth/Nation, 2002), ix.

10 Noam Chomsky, *9-11* (New York: Seven Stories, 2002), 118.

11 Gore Vidal, "Menandering towards Armageddon," reprinted in *Dreaming War*, 57–68.

12 On the homogenization of U.S. television coverage of the War in Iraq, see Michael Massing, "The Unseen War," *New York Review of Books*, May 29, 2003, 16–19.

Index

Marcie Frank is a professor of English at Concordia
University. She is the author of *Gender, Theatre, and the
Origins of Criticism from Dryden to Manley* (2002).

Library of Congress Cataloging-in-Publication Data
Frank, Marcie.
How to be an intellectual in the age of TV :
the lessons of Gore Vidal / Marcie Frank.
p. cm. — (Public planet books)
Includes bibliographical references and index.
ISBN 0–8223–3602–2 (acid-free paper)
ISBN 0–8223–3640–5 (pbk. : acid-free paper)
1. Vidal, Gore, 1925—Knowledge and learning.
2. United States—Intellectual life—20th century.
3. Television personalities—United States.
4. Intellectuals—United States. I. Title. II. Series.
PS3543.I26Z66 2005
818′.5409—dc22   2005008863